It's another Quality Book from CGP

This book is for anyone doing GCSE French at Foundation Level.

It contains lots of tricky questions designed
to make you sweat — because that's the only
way you'll get any better.

It's also got some daft bits in to try and make
the whole experience at least vaguely
entertaining for you.

What CGP is all about

Our sole aim here at CGP is to produce the highest quality
books — carefully written, immaculately presented and
dangerously close to being funny.

Then we work our socks off to get them out to you
— at the cheapest possible prices.

Contents

SECTION ONE — TOPICS

SECTION TWO — GRAMMAR

Published by Coordination Group Publications Ltd.

Contributors:
Angela Billington
Simon Cook
Taissa Csàky
Gemma Hallam
Katherine Stewart
Nadia Waller

Monsieur LeBoeuf was not harmed in the making of this book.

ISBN: 1 84146 804 5

With thanks to Sophie Lavarene for the proofreading.

Groovy website: www.cgpbooks.co.uk

Jolly bits of clipart from CorelDRAW

Printed by Elanders Hindson, Newcastle upon Tyne.

Numbers

Q1   Write out these French numbers in figures.

The words for numbers are dead important. You **won't** get away without knowing them.

eg *quatre* ⟹ **4**

a) quatre   d) dix-huit

b) neuf   e) vingt

c) onze   f) quatorze

Q2   Write out these numbers as words (in French).

eg   *1* ⟹ *un*   *31* ⟹ *trente et un*   *102* ⟹ *cent deux*

a) 1	e) 109	i) 63	m) 1983
b) 7	f) 35	j) 581	n) 2004
c) 8	g) 17	k) 392	o) 1999
d) 14	h) 71	l) 5431	p) 1 000 000

Useful words: un million = 1 million   mille = 1 thousand
soixante-dix = 70   quatre-vingts = 80   quatre-vingt-dix = 90

Q3   Write out these "one, two, three" numbers as "first, second, third" etc.

eg *deux* ⟹ *deuxième*   *vingt* ⟹ *vingtième*

a) dix   d) deux

b) sept   e) quatre-vingts

c) un   f) deux cents

Watch out for 'un' — it isn't what you'd expect. Just think 'premier league'...

Q4   Write out the price on each ticket in French.   eg a) €125 = *cent vingt-cinq euros*

a)
€125,00

b) € 89,50

c) € 210

d) PRIX SPÉCIAL
F 149,95

Careful — the French use <u>commas</u> instead of decimal points. This price ticket says 89 euros and 50 cents.

Useful Words

Q1   Write out all the French words a) to h) along with the right English translation from the box.

eg quelques ⟹ some

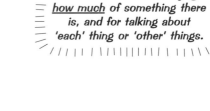

These words are for saying *how much* of something there is, and for talking about 'each' thing or 'other' things.

a) quelques
b) plusieurs
c) chaque
d) tous les

e) beaucoup de
f) toutes les
g) peu de
h) d'autres

some	all the (feminine)	few	several every/each
others	all the (masculine)		many/a lot of

Q2   Turn each French sentence below into English and write it out.

eg Chaque homme porte un chapeau. ⟹ Every man is wearing a hat.

a) Chaque homme porte un chapeau.
b) Tous les supermarchés sont ouverts le dimanche.
c) J'ai vu beaucoup de jeunes au centre commercial.
d) Il est venu avec quelques amis.
e) J'ai lu ce livre plusieurs fois.

Use the words from Q1 to help you here.

Q3   Write out each French word a) to d) along with the matching English one from the box.

eg a) souvent ⟹ often

a) souvent   c) quelquefois
b) rarement   d) toujours

always	often	sometimes	rarely

Q4   Put these sentences into French, using the vocab on this page, and write them out in full.

a) I sometimes play the guitar.   b) I often eat pizza.

Look up any words you don't know.

Questions

Q1   Match up these English question words with the right French ones from the circle. Write them out together.

eg When ➡ *Quand*

a) When

b) Why

c) Where

d) Who

e) How

f) How many/much

g) What

h) Which

Combien

Quand   Quels

Pourquoi   Comment

Qu'est-ce que

Qui   Où

Q2   Turn each of these French questions into English ones.

eg *Est-ce que tu as des frères ou des soeurs?* ➡ *Do you have any brothers or sisters?*

a) Est-ce que tu as des frères ou des soeurs?

b) Comment allez-vous?

c) Qu'est-ce que tu fais demain soir?

d) Il y a combien de pommes ici?

e) Où est mon pantalon?

f) Il va arriver à quelle heure?

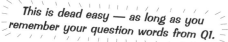

This is dead easy — as long as you remember your question words from Q1.

Helpful words:	*les frères* = brothers *demain* = tomorrow
	les pommes = apples *le pantalon* = trousers

Q3   Fill in the gaps in each question with the right French word from the box.

eg (when) ➡ *Quand est-ce que le film commence?*

a) .... est-ce que le film commence?   (*when*)

b) .... sont mes chaussettes?   (*where*)

c) .... tu aimes faire le soir?   (*what*)

d) .... peut me donner un stylo?   (*who*)

e) .... est-ce que tu chantes ces chansons?   (*why*)

Pourquoi

Qui   **Où**

Qu'est-ce que

Quand

French Rubrics

Rubrics just mean 'Exam instructions'.

Q1 Write out these bits of rubric and put what they mean, too.

eg *Lisez la liste.* ⟹ *Read the list.*

a) Lisez la liste.

b) Répondez aux questions.

c) Tournez la page.

d) Voici un exemple.

e) Répondez en français.

f) D'abord, ...

Q2 Turn these bits of French rubric into English — just match up
each French phrase a) to i) with the right English bit from the box.

eg *Écrivez la lettre du mot qui correspond à l'illustration.*
⟹ *Write the letter of the word that matches the picture.*

a) Écrivez la lettre du mot qui correspond à l'illustration.

b) Trouvez le symbole qui correspond au mot.

c) Vous n'aurez pas besoin de toutes les lettres.

d) Vous pouvez employer un dictionnaire si vous voulez.

Some questions in the exams'll be in French — so you'll need to get these rubrics drilled into your brain.

e) Dessinez une flèche pour montrer quelle illustration va avec quel panneau.

f) Remplissez la grille.

g) Répondez en français ou cochez les cases.

h) Cochez les cases appropriées.

i) Regardez la grille.

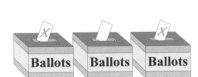

Draw an arrow to show which picture goes with which caption.

Fill in the grid.   Answer in French or tick the boxes.

Look at the grid.   Find the symbol that goes with the word.

You won't need all the letters.   Tick the right boxes.

Write the letter of the word that matches the picture.

You can use a dictionary if you want to.

Informal Letters

Q1 Read this letter and answer the questions underneath in English.

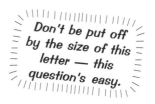

Don't be put off by the size of this letter — this question's easy.

> La Rochelle, le 23 octobre
>
> Salut!
>
> Merci de ta lettre. Je suis très content d'avoir un correspondant anglais.
>
> Eh bien, moi, j'ai quinze ans. J'habite un appartement au centre de La Rochelle avec mes parents et ma soeur, Martine. Mon père est agent de police et ma mère est dentiste.
>
> Je vais au collège St Étienne, à La Rochelle. Mes matières préférées sont la physique et la géographie. Je déteste les maths parce que c'est très difficiles et mon prof est trop strict.
>
> J'aime beaucoup le football. Mon équipe préférée est Bordeaux. Quelle est ton équipe préférée? J'espère recevoir bientôt de tes nouvelles.
> Amitiés,
>
> Gérard

a) What does 'Salut' mean?

b) How old does Gérard say he is?

c) What is Gérard's sister called?

d) What does Gérard's father do?

e) What does Gérard's mother do?

f) What are Gérard's favourite subjects?

g) Why does Gérard say he hates maths?

h) Who is Gérard's favourite football team?

Give short answers — you don't need whole sentences.

Tricky words:
correspondant = pen pal
le collège = secondary school
les matières = subjects
la physique = physics
l'équipe = team
J'espère = I hope
bientôt = soon
les nouvelles = news

Q2 Write a short letter in French that covers all the stuff below.

- Put 'Dear Gérard'. Thank him for his letter.
- Say you are 15 years old.
- Tell him where you live.
- Tell him which your favourite football team is.
- Say that you hope to receive his news soon.

BIG HINT: You just need to find the right phrases from Gérard's letter in Q1.

Remember — you get marks for getting the layout right: address, date, name and all that.

6

Instructions and Being Polite

Q1   Turn these French instructions a) to i) into English ones.
The list of verbs underneath is there to help you.

You've probably heard some of these phrases in the classroom.

eg   *Levez-vous!* ➡ *Get up!*

a)   Levez-vous!

b)   Asseyez-vous!

c)   Tais-toi!

d)   Taisez-vous!

e)   Donnez-moi votre cahier.

f)   Prête-moi ton stylo.

g)   Écoutez-moi!

h)   Écrivez ça dans votre cahier.

i)   Arrêtez!

List of Verbs

(se) lever = to get up   prêter = to lend
(s') asseoir = to sit down   écouter = to listen
(se) taire = to stop talking   écrire = to write
donner = to give   arrêter = to stop

Sergeant Burt liked to show his
deadly finger to new recruits.

Q2   Work out what you'd say in each situation a) to f). Pick the
right French phrase from the box for each one and write it out.

eg   *You want to stop a man in the street to ask for directions.*

➡ ***Excusez-moi, monsieur.***

Think before you pick — make sure you only use each phrase ONCE.

a)   You want to stop a man in the street to ask for directions.

b)   You've spilt coffee on your best mate's favourite sweater.

c)   You're saying "How are you?" to someone you don't know that well.

d)   Someone's just thanked you for something, and you want to say it's OK.

e)   You're in a china shop, and you've accidentally broken a load of plates.

f)   You've just been introduced to a charming lady.

Watch out! If you're a girl you need to put an extra 'e' on some words — eg 'enchantée' or 'je suis désolée'.

Je m'excuse!   Enchanté(e)   Excusez-moi, monsieur.
        De rien.   Comment allez-vous?   Je suis désolé(e)

__Opinions__

Q1 Tick the right box to show if each of the phrases a) to h) means you *like* or *dislike* something.

The first one's done for you.

Like   Dislike

a) J'aime .....   ✔   ☐

b) .... me plaît.   ☐   ☐

c) ...... ne m'intéresse pas.   ☐   ☐

d) Je trouve .... affreux.   ☐   ☐

e) J'aime bien ....   ☐   ☐

f) ...., ça va.   ☐   ☐

g) Je la trouve sympa.   ☐   ☐

h) Je m'intéresse à .....   ☐   ☐

Q2 Claudine is droning on to her friend Max about what she thinks of her family and friends.
Pick the right word from the box to finish each of her sentences, then write them out in full.

eg **Max: Qu'est-ce que tu penses de tes petites nièces?**

Claudine: Elles sont .... (pretty)   ➡   **Elles sont belles.**

It's dead easy — just pick the right word.

belles

formidable

ennuyeuse   gentil

affreux

Remember: avis = opinion.

Max: Quel est ton avis sur Charles?
Claudine: Je trouve Charles ....   (kind)

Max: Qu'est-ce que tu penses de Laurent?
Claudine: Je trouve Laurent ....   (awful)

Max: Qu'est-ce que tu penses de Sophie?
Claudine: Je trouve Sophie ....   (boring)

Max: Quel est ton avis sur Jean-Pierre?
Claudine: Je le trouve ....   (great)

Opinions

Q1 Write out each English word a) to f) along with the matching French word from the box.

eg beautiful ⟹ beau/belle

a) beautiful
b) interesting
c) great
d) excellent
e) bad
f) friendly

mauvais(e)
chouette
beau/belle
intéressant(e)
amical(e)
excellent(e)

Q2 This bit's all about saying what you think of things. Write a full sentence answer in French for each question a) to d) using one of the words from the box.

eg Qu'est-ce que tu penses du sport? ⟹ Je pense que le sport est chouette.

What do you think of sport?   I think sport is great.

a) Qu'est-ce que tu penses du sport?
b) Qu'est-ce que tu penses de mon ami?
c) Qu'est-ce que tu penses du jazz?
d) Qu'est-ce que tu penses de l'art moderne?

Qu'est-ce que vous pensez de l'art moderne?

C'est m***e

chouette   sympa   ennuyeux   affreux

Q3 The sentences a) to d) are things people have said. In the box there's a list of reasons. Match up each sentence with the right reason, and write them out together.

eg Je trouve les OuestBoyz excellents ⟹ parce qu'ils chantent bien.

a) Je trouve les OuestBoyz excellents
b) Jean-Pierre est fatigué
c) Je ne peux pas sortir ce soir
d) Marie ne va pas acheter ces chaussures

parce que j'ai trop de devoirs à faire.
parce qu'ils chantent bien.
parce qu'elles sont trop chères.
parce qu'il a beaucoup travaillé.

_Tricky words: devoirs = homework   travailler = to work
acheter = to buy   les chaussures = shoes   fatigué = tired_

The Weather

Q1 Look at each picture a) to f) and pick the right French phrase 1) to 6) that goes with it.

a)

eg 4) il y a des nuages

b)

c)

d)

e)

f)

1) il pleut   2) il fait du soleil   3) il neige

4) il y a des nuages   5) il fait beau   6) il fait du vent

Q2 Write out each of the French weather phrases a) to f) below.
Pick the right English translation from the box and write it out alongside.

eg Il pleut ⟹ It's raining.

a) Il pleut.   c) Il y a des éclairs.   e) Il fait froid.

b) Il fait du vent.   d) Il fait beau.   f) Il fait chaud.

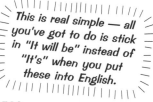

> **It is fine.   It's windy.   It's raining.**
> **It's cold.   There's lightning.   It's hot.**

Q3 Put these French weather sentences about the future into English.

This is real simple — all you've got to do is stick in "It will be" instead of "It's" when you put these into English.

eg Il fera beau. ⟹ It will be fine.

a) Il fera froid.   c) Il fera du soleil.   e) Il y aura des nuages.

b) Il fera du vent.   d) Il neigera.   f) Il pleuvra.

Q4 Put these French weather sentences about the past into English.

eg Il neigeait. ⟹ It was snowing.

a) Il faisait du soleil.   c) Il faisait mauvais.   e) Il pleuvait.

b) Il y avait du brouillard.   d) Il faisait beau.   f) Il y avait des éclairs.

Countries

Q1 Pick the right French names from the box for each country below, then write them out.

Italy   the Netherlands   Wales   Northern Ireland
Austria   Spain   Germany   America
Africa   England   the United States France
Scotland   Europe   Belgium   Great Britain

l'Italie   l'Angleterre

l'Irlande du Nord   l'Allemagne

l'Autriche   l'Afrique

l'Europe   la France

la Grande-Bretagne   l'Espagne

l'Écosse   le pays de Galles

l'Amérique   la Belgique

les Pays-Bas   les États-Unis

Q2 Write out in French what you'd say if you came from each country a) to f).
Pick the right word from the box underneath to help you.

eg Italy ⟹ **Je suis italien/Je suis italienne.**
I am Italian.

Remember — NO capital at the start of words like 'italien'.

a) Ireland   c) Scotland   e) Germany
b) the Netherlands d) England   f) Wales

Don't forget to stick the extra 'e' on if you're a girl.

allemand(e)   irlandais(e)   gallois(e)
anglais(e)   écossais(e)   hollandais(e)

Q3 Write out the answers to these questions in French.

a) Quelle est votre nationalité?   *eg Je suis français.*
b) D'où venez-vous?   **Je viens de la France.**

Je viens... = I come from...

Hotels and Hostels

Q1   This question's all about hotel vocab. Write out each of the French words below.
Pick the matching English word for each one from the grey circle and write it out too.

partir   la demi-pension   rester

la pension complète   une chambre simple   la personne

la nuit   une auberge   le camping

                                                       réserver

                                                       coûter

to reserve
single room   guest house
youth hostel   campsite
                   full board
night
hotel   to stay   holidays
     space available
  to cost   half board
person   to leave
   double room

une auberge de jeunesse

les vacances

la chambre double

la place

un hôtel

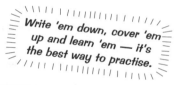

Write 'em down, cover 'em up and learn 'em — it's the best way to practise.

Q2   Read this sign about a youth hostel and answer the questions in English.

AUBERGE DE JEUNESSE CAEN

Nous offrons:
huit chambres doubles, avec douche
cinq chambres simples, avec douche
seize chambres à huit personnes, salle de bains commune.

Pour réserver votre lit appelez le 025 85 47 62 35.
Si vous ne vous présentez pas à l'auberge avant 22h00, votre lit peut être offert à d'autres.

---

a)   How many double bedrooms with showers are there?

b)   How many single bedrooms with showers are there?

c)   How many people are the other sixteen rooms for?

d)   What does it say about the bathroom?

Camping

Q1   Read these signs from a French campsite. Write out what they mean in English.

a)

**Bienvenue aux
Champs du Soleil**
*emplacements
pour 30 tentes et 15 caravanes*

b)
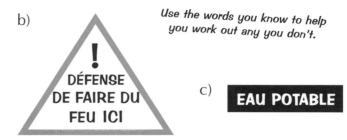

*Use the words you know to help
you work out any you don't.*

**!
DÉFENSE
DE FAIRE DU
FEU ICI**

c)   **EAU POTABLE**

d)
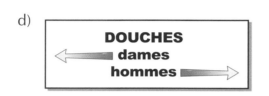

DOUCHES
dames
hommes

e)   *On peut louer des sacs de couchage ici.*

Q2   Read this conversation about campsites, then pick **A**, **B** or **C** to answer each question.

> **Élise:**   Excusez-moi, monsieur — nous restons au terrain de camping **Mille Plaisirs** près de la plage. Où restez-vous?
>
> **Bertrand:**   Je suis depuis dimanche au **Camping Bonnes Vacances**. Il est loin de la plage, mais il est très joli.
>
> **Cyril:**   Vraiment? Nous n'aimons pas notre terrain. Il y a trop de petits enfants.
>
> **Bertrand:**   Insupportable! Nous allons tous ensemble au **Camping Bonnes Vacances**. Il y a bien sûr un emplacement là-bas pour votre tente.
>
> **Élise:**   Nous avons une caravane — est-ce qu'il y a des emplacements pour les caravanes aussi?
>
> **Bertrand:**   Bien sûr! Allons-y!

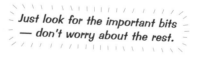
Just look for the important bits — don't worry about the rest.

How about 4 nights, Hot Lips?

a) Where is Élise staying?

A a campsite on the beach   **B** a campsite in the village   **C** a campsite near the beach

b) What does Bertrand say about the place where he's staying?

A it's only open on Sundays   **B** he's been staying since Sunday   **C** he's leaving on Sunday

c) What doesn't Cyril like about the campsite where he's staying?

A there are too many dogs   **B** there are too many small children   **C** there are no toilets

d) What does Élise ask Bertrand about the Bonnes Vacances campsite?

A if there are toilets   **B** if there are car-parking spaces   **C** if there are caravan places

More on Hotels

Q1   Bernice is staying in a posh hotel in France. Read the list of questions she asks the receptionist, and pick the right English version **A** or **B**.

a) Où est la salle à manger, s'il vous plaît?

    A Where is the sitting room, please?   **B** Where is the dining room, please?

b) À quel étage est ma chambre?

    A What floor is my bedroom on?   **B** What floor is my bathroom on?

c) Est-ce que je peux voir la piscine de ma fenêtre?

    A Can I see the fishing port from my room? **B** Can I see the pool from my room?

d) Où est le parking s'il vous plaît?

    A Where is the car park please? **B** Where is the bar please?

Q2   The receptionist drones on a bit about the rules of the hotel.
Read what he says, then answer the questions below in English.

"Maintenant, il est deux heures et quart, et la salle à manger est fermée. Mais si vous voulez quelque chose, par exemple du café et un sandwich, je peux l'envoyer à votre chambre.

*   La salle à manger est ouverte pour le petit déjeuner entre sept heures et demie et dix heures. Si vous ne vous levez pas avant dix heures, le déjeuner est servi entre midi et quinze heures. Quand vous quittez l'hôtel, il faut quitter la chambre avant onze heures."*

a) What time does the receptionist say it is now?

b) Is the dining room open now?

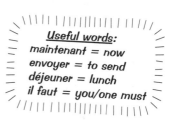

Useful words:
maintenant = now
envoyer = to send
déjeuner = lunch
il faut = you/one must

c) What does the receptionist say he could send to Bernice's room?

d) What time do they start and finish serving breakfast?

e) What time do they start and finish serving lunch?

f) What time do you have to leave your room if you're leaving the hotel?

Buildings

Q1   Write down the French names for each of these places a) to p) using the box to help you.

eg a) *la boucherie*

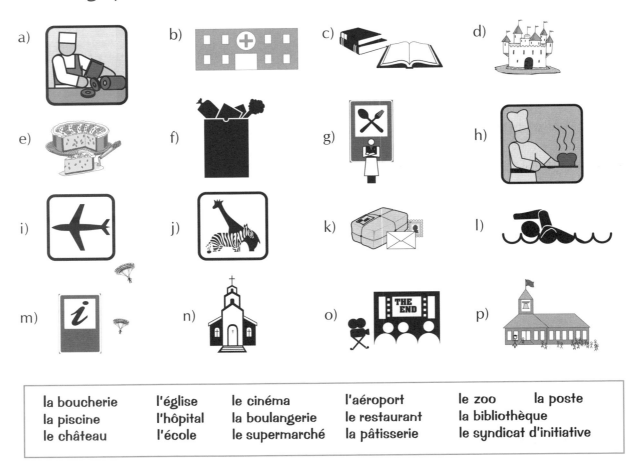

la boucherie	l'église	le cinéma	l'aéroport	le zoo	la poste
la piscine	l'hôpital	la boulangerie	le restaurant	la bibliothèque	
le château	l'école	le supermarché	la pâtisserie	le syndicat d'initiative	

Q2   Write out each of the French sentences a) to d) filling in the gaps
with one of the places or buildings from the box below.

Look up any words you don't know.

à la banque	au théâtre
au musée	une pharmacie

eg *Je vais .... pour changer de l'argent.* ➡ *Je vais à la banque pour changer de l'argent.*

a) Je vais .... pour changer de l'argent.

Don't give stupid answers — choose a place that fits with the sentence.

b) Hier soir, j'ai vu une très jolie pièce ....

c) On peut voir les objets très vieux faits par les gens d'autrefois ....

d) Je voudrais acheter de l'aspirine. Est-ce qu'il y a .... près d'ici?

Tourist Information

Q1   Élise and Cyrille are looking for the local museum. Pick the
      question a), b) or c) that's most likely to get them helpful directions.

a)   Pour aller au château, s'il vous plaît?

b)   Est-ce qu'il y a une confiserie près d'ici?

c)   Où est le musée, s'il vous plaît?

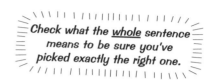

Check what the whole sentence means to be sure you've picked exactly the right one.

Q2   What should they say if they want to ask if the museum's far away? Pick a), b) or c).

a)   Le musée, c'est ouvert aujourd'hui?

b)   Est-ce que le musée est loin d'ici?

c)   Est-ce qu'il y a un musée près d'ici?

Q3   The tourist office gives Cyrille and Élise a print-out with directions to the museum.
      Read it through carefully, then answer the questions below in English.

> Syndicat d'initiative
> **St. Julien**
> *Le Musée des Huîtres Françaises*
>
> Vous vous trouvez maintenant au syndicat d'initiative de la petite ville de St.
> Julien. Sortez du bureau, et vous vous trouvez sur la Place de la Ville.
> Prenez la Rue Sainte Mathilde, qui commence à gauche de la mairie. Suivez
> cette rue jusqu'aux feux. Tournez à droite ici et continuez tout droit devant le
> Café Delphine. Au coin vous trouvez le Musée des Huîtres Françaises.
>
> Amusez-vous bien à St. Julien!

Helpful words:
la mairie = town hall   le coin = corner
gauche = left   les feux = lights
droite = right   tout droit = straight on
se trouver = to find yourself
le syndicat d'initiative = tourist office

a)   On what square is the St. Julien tourist information office?

b)   What major building will you need to help you find the Rue Sainte Mathilde?

c)   How far should you follow the Rue Sainte Mathilde?

d)   Which direction do you go in when you turn out of the Rue Sainte Mathilde?

e)   Should you change direction when you get to the Café Delphine?

f)   Where will you find the Musée des Huîtres Françaises?*

les huîtres = oysters

Tourist Information

Q1 Write sentences in French asking for information about each of the places or things a) to f).

This is a cinch — all you have to do is stick the same phrase onto everything.

eg **a) le théâtre** **Pouvez-vous me donner des informations sur le théâtre?**

Can you give me some information about the theatre?

a) le théâtre

b) le zoo

c) l'exposition dans le musée

d) les attractions de la ville

e) les autobus

f) les vélos à louer*

*bikes to hire

Q2 Here are a bunch of signs showing when some local shops and museums are open or closed. Write full sentences in French to answer the questions a) to g).

DECLERC
heures d'ouverture
Du lundi au samedi: 8h - 22h
Dimanche:
9h - 18h

Confiserie 'Marie-Anne'
Ouverte du lundi au vendredi
8h - 16h

Bibliothèque
heures d'ouverture
du lundi au vendredi
10h - 19h
samedi 10h - 14h

Musée de l'archéologie
ouvert:
du mardi au vendredi 8h - 20h
samedi et dimanche 9h - 13h
fermé: lundi

eg **Quand ouvre la bibliothèque?**  **La bibliothèque ouvre à dix heures.**

When does the library open? The library opens at 10 o'clock.

a) Quand ouvre la bibliothèque?

b) Quand ouvre la confiserie, le jeudi?

c) Quand ouvre le supermarché *Declerc*, le lundi?

d) Quand ferme le supermarché *Declerc*, le dimanche?

e) Quand ferme la confiserie?

f) Quand ferme le musée d'archéologie le dimanche?

g) Quels jours est-ce que la confiserie est ouverte?

Give the times as full numbers.

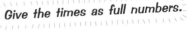

Pour aller à la Poissonnerie?

Day Trips

Q1   At the Tourist Information Office in Tours, you see a poster listing the day trips you can do by coach. Answer the questions below (no need for full sentences).

EXCURSIONS EN CAR

Où	Attraction	Jours	Départ	Prix/ prix enfants
Blois	château	mercredi, dimanche	10h	€5/€2,5
Poitiers	les cinémas de l'avenir	mardi, jeudi	9h	€6/€3
Chenonceaux	château, jardins	mardi, mercredi	9h (mardi) 10h (mercredi)	€6,5/€3,25
Chaumont	château	jeudi, dimanche	9h, 11h	€6/€3
Onzain	vins de la région	samedi	10h30	€5,5/€2,75
Paris	Tour Eiffel, Île de France	vendredi	8h30	€15/€7,5

a)   Where would you go to see the latest cinema technology?

b)   Which of the chateaux has got gardens?

c)   What drink can you try in Onzain?

d)   Which trips only happen once a week?

e)   Who pays the cheaper price for each excursion?

f)   Where can you go on a Wednesday?

g)   Which place has two coaches going to it on the same day?

h)   On what day are there no excursions?

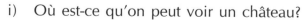

i)   Où est-ce qu'on peut voir un château?

j)   Quelle excursion est la plus chère?

k)   Où est-ce qu'on peut aller le dimanche?

l)   Où est-ce qu'on va pour goûter du vin?

m) Où est-ce qu'on peut aller le mardi, à 9 heures?

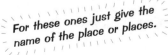
For these ones just give the name of the place or places.

Holidays

Q1 Write a sentence in French saying where each person went on holiday.

> eg Xavier — Angleterre ➡ *Xavier est allé en Angleterre.*
> Marie — Irlande *Marie est allée en Irlande.*

If the person is female, you'll need an extra 'e' on 'allé'.

a) Pascal — Suède   Francis — Italie   Jean-Philippe — Écosse

b) Sophie — États-Unis   Mathilde — Espagne   Antoinette — France

est allé(e) = went

Q2 Four people were asked where they went on holiday and what they did. Use the table to answer the questions a) to j) below.

	Où es-tu allé(e)?	Avec qui?	Pour combien de temps?	Comment tu y es allé(e)?	Qu'est-ce que tu as fait?
Matthieu	Bretagne	Ma famille	quinze jours	en voiture	plage, tennis
Jacqueline	Allemagne	Mes copines	trois semaines	en train	châteaux, randonnées
Alice	Grèce	Mon père, ma mère, mon frère	dix jours	en avion	plage, ruines
Blaise	Angleterre	Mon copain	deux semaines	en bateau	concert, tennis

Watch out — remember Bretagne means Brittany.

Write the answers in English.

a) Who went to a concert on holiday?

b) Who went by plane?

c) How long did Matthieu go to Brittany for?

d) Who went to Greece with Alice?

e) How did Jacqueline travel to Germany?

f) What did Alice do in Greece?

g) What did Blaise do in England?

h) Who did Blaise go on holiday with?

i) How did Blaise get to England?

j) Who went away for two weeks?

Alice realised cut-price air travel had reached new lows.

Holidays

Q1   Read these postcards and answer the questions a) to n) in English.

---

mercredi 14 juillet

Cher Claude,
Je suis allé en Espagne, il y a deux semaines. C'était fantastique! Il faisait chaud, alors je suis allé à la plage chaque jour. J'ai joué au volley et au tennis. Je me suis beaucoup amusé.
Amitiés,
Pierre

Chère Analise,   lundi 23 août
Comment étaient mes vacances à Cornwall? Je ne les ai pas aimées. J'étais en vacances avec ma famille. Nous y sommes allés en voiture et mon frère s'est senti malade. Puis il a plu toute la semaine. L'année prochaine, je vais aller en vacances en Amérique toute seule!
À bientôt,
Sophie

Wish you were here...

Cher Max,   2 octobre
Salut! Quelles vacances! J'étais à Bognor avec Marilyn, pendant un mois. Je me suis détendu. Il y avait du vent et il neigeait, mais ce n'était pas un problème. Nous restions au camping de Butlins, alors il y avait beaucoup de choses à faire. Chaque nuit je suis allé à la discothèque, et je me suis amusé. J'adore le Butlins!
À bientôt,
Elvis

> _Blimey — this is a bit tougher, so take your time and make sure you answer the questions properly._

a)   Did Pierre enjoy his holiday?

b)   Who did Sophie go on holiday with?

c)   Did Sophie enjoy her holiday?

d)   Where did Elvis go?

e)   How did Sophie get to Cornwall?

f)   Where did Elvis and Marilyn stay?

g)   What was the weather like in Spain?

h)   How was Elvis' holiday?

i)   What was the weather like in Bognor?

j)   What did Pierre do in Spain?

k)   Does Elvis like Butlins?

l)   Where did Pierre go every day?

m) How long was Sophie on holiday?

n)   Where does Sophie want to go next year?

Holidays

Q1   Here's a list of questions a) to f) and a box with all the answers muddled up.
     Write out each question, then pick the right answer and write it out alongside.

eg Qu'est-ce que tu vas faire demain? ➡ Demain, je vais voir un match de football.

What are you going to do tomorrow?   Tomorrow, I'm going to watch a football match.

a)   Qu'est-ce que tu vas faire demain?

b)   Tu iras en vacances avec qui?

c)   Comment tu iras en Floride?

d)   Où est-ce que tu vas aller en vacances cette année?

e)   Qu'est-ce que tu feras?

f)   Tu iras pour combien de temps?

> *J'irai avec ma soeur.*
> *Je vais aller en Floride en avion.*
> *Demain, je vais voir un match de football.*
> *Je vais aller aux États-Unis cette année.*
> *J'irai pour trois semaines.*
> *Je vais aller à Disneyworld.*

Remember there's only one really right answer for each question.

Q2   Look at the people and places listed below in French.
     Write a sentence in French for each person like the example.

You'll need to use 'va aller' or 'ira' for these sentences.

eg Jean — aux Pays-Bas ➡ Jean va aller aux Pays-Bas.

Jean is going to go to Holland.

Jean — aux Pays-Bas   Françoise — en Russie   Nicole — en Italie   Luc — en Suisse

Marie — en Allemagne   Gérald — au Danemark   David — en France

Q3   Here's a list of people, places and types of transport. Answer the question below in French.

Comment ils iront?

eg   Bill — en Irlande; en bateau ➡ Bill va aller en Irlande en bateau.

Bill is going to Ireland by boat.

Bill — en Irlande; en bateau   Sylvie — en Grèce; en avion

Jacques — en Belgique; en vélo   Edouard — en Autriche; en voiture

Where You Live

Q1   Answer the questions below using the information on this map of France.

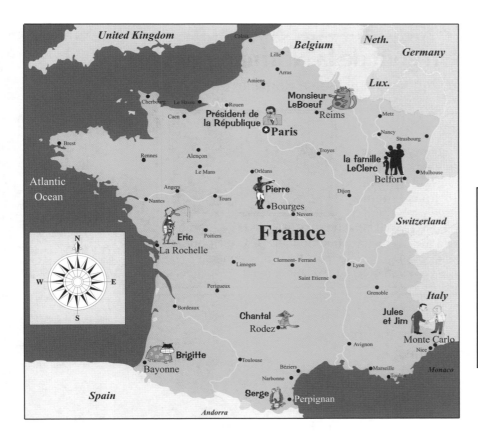

LA BOUSSOLE

north:	le nord
east:	l'est
south:	le sud
west:	l'ouest
south-east:	le sud-est
south-west:	le sud-ouest
north-east:	le nord-est
north-west:	le nord-ouest

la boussole = compass

a)   Write full sentences in French to answer these questions.

> **eg Où habite Serge?** ⟹ **Serge habite à Perpignan.**
>
> Where does Serge live?   Serge lives in Perpignan.

Où habite Serge?   Où habite Chantal?   Où habite Monsieur LeBoeuf?

Où habite Brigitte?   Où habitent Jules et Jim?   Où habite le Président de la République?

b)   Answer these questions with full French sentences too.

> **eg Où se trouve Le Havre?** ⟹ **Le Havre se trouve dans le nord-ouest de la France.**
>
> Where is Le Havre situated?   Le Havre is situated in the North-West of France.

Où se trouve Paris?   Où se trouve La Rochelle?

Où se trouve Nice?   Où se trouve Toulouse?

Où se trouve Caen?   Où se trouve Strasbourg?

Use the list of direction words beside the map to help you.

Where You Live

Q1 Here's a newspaper interview about Bogville.
Read it through and answer the questions below.

Bogville: Un goût de la Normandie
France Aujourd'hui — Bienvenue à Bogville.

Journaliste: *"Qu'est-ce qu'il y a faire dans ta ville?"*

Olivier: Vivre à Bogville, c'est un peu ennuyeux. Il n'y a rien à faire pour les jeunes ici. Il y a quelquefois des fêtes folkloriques, mais d'habitude c'est une ville très calme. Les jeunes préféreraient vivre dans une ville plus grande avec un ciné et des boîtes de nuit. Tu sais, les jeunes gens ne s'intéressent pas

beaucoup aux marchés traditionnels. C'est pour les vieux, tout ça. J'aimerais vivre à Paris ou à Londres, peut-être.

Useful Words:
rien = nothing
fêtes folkloriques = traditional fairs
les boîtes de nuit = nightclubs
les marchés = markets
les vieux = old people

a) Write out these sentences from the interview and fill in the bits that are missing:

Piece of cake — the answers are all there if you read the article carefully.

Vivre à **Bogville**, c'est un peu ....

Il y a quelquefois des ...., mais d'habitude c'est une ville très calme.

Les jeunes préféreraient vivre dans .... et des boîtes de nuit.

Tu sais, les jeunes gens .... beaucoup aux marchés traditionnels.

C'est pour les ...., tout ça.

J'aimerais .... ou à Londres, peut-être.

b) Complétez le table: vrai (**V**) ou faux (**F**).*

Olivier aime vivre à Bogville.	F	Bogville se trouve en Normandie.	
Vivre à Bogville, c'est intéressant.		Il n'y a rien à faire pour les jeunes.	
D'habitude c'est une ville calme.		Il y a des fêtes folkloriques.	
Les jeunes n'aiment pas vivre à Bogville.		Olivier aimerait vivre à Toulouse.	

*vrai = true   faux = false

Trains

Q1   Write out the French train words below along with the matching English words from the box.

l'arrivée   un aller simple   le départ   partir   deuxième classe

quai   changer   le chemin de fer   un aller et retour

departure	arrival	railway	change trains	single ticket
leave	second class	return ticket	platform	

Q2   Read this conversation at a ticket office and answer the questions in English.

Madge:	Est-ce qu'il y a un train pour Paris ce soir, s'il vous plaît?
Attendant:	Oui, Mademoiselle. Il y a deux trains pour Paris ce soir.
	À quelle heure voulez-vous partir?
Madge:	Je voudrais partir à vingt heures.
Attendant:	Ah, il y a un train à vingt heures trente.
Madge:	Excellent! Un aller et retour pour Paris, s'il vous plaît.
Attendant:	Oui, Mademoiselle. En quelle classe?
Madge:	Deuxième classe, s'il vous plaît.
Attendant:	Voilà. Le train part du quai numéro cinq.
Madge:	Merci beaucoup.

Remember:
vingt heures = 8pm.

a)   How many trains are there for Paris?

b)   What time does Madge want to leave?

c)   When does the attendant say there's a train?

d)   What kind of ticket does Madge ask for?

e)   What class does Madge want to travel?

f)   What platform does the train leave from?

Q3   Turn these English sentences into French ones.

At 6 Mr Bond?
No, I really don't think
that will be possible.

BOILING
OIL

eg There's a train at half-past ten. ⟹ *Il y a un train à dix heures et demie.*

There's a train at half-past ten.

A return ticket to Toulouse please.

Is there a train for Caen this evening?

The train is leaving from platform 3.

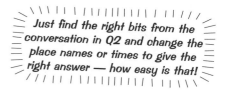

Just find the right bits from the conversation in Q2 and change the place names or times to give the right answer — how easy is that!

Trains

Q1   Write out each French word a) to l) along with the matching English words from the box.

a) l'horaire

b) le guichet

c) la salle d'attente

d) non-fumeurs

e) la consigne

f) monter dans

g) la gare

h) arriver

i) le billet

j) fumeurs

k) le retard

l) descendre de

| station | to get on | no-smoking | left-luggage office | waiting room | ticket |
| timetable | delay | ticket window | to arrive | smoking | to get off |

These letters tell you what days the trains run on.

Q2   Read this timetable and answer the questions about it below.

	a	b	a	c	b	d
Paris	08.00	08.15	09.00	10.50	12.00	12.50
Orléans	08.05	08.25	09.15	10.00	11.30	13.00
Blois	07.58	08.45	09.30	10.35	11.40	12.35
Lyons	08.10	08.55	09.40	10.20	11.15	12.20

LÉGENDE
a: du lundi au samedi
b: tous les jours
c: le weekend seulement
d: le dimanche seulement

a) What does 'du lundi au samedi' mean in English?

b) What does 'tous les jours' mean?

c) What time is the train to Paris on Sunday only?

d) What time is the first train to Orléans on Monday?

e) You want to go to Blois on Tuesday after 10 o'clock am. What time is the first train?

f) You want to go to Lyons between 10 am and 12 on Saturday. How many trains are there?

g) You want to go to Paris on Sunday between 11 and 1 pm (13). How many trains are there?

h) You want to go to Orléans on Wednesday. It's 10.30 am. What time is the first train?

i) You want to go to Paris on Friday. It's 10.30 am. What time is the first train?

j) You want to go to Blois on Saturday. It's 9.50 am. What time is the first train?

k) You want to go to Lyons on Thursday. It's 8.30 am. What time is the first train?

Watch out for these — make sure you check which days each train runs on.

Other Transport

Q1 Write out what each of these types of transport is in English?   *eg en camion = by lorry*

a) en bus   d) en car   g) en moto

b) en vélo   e) en bateau   h) en métro

c) en voiture   f) en avion   i)) à pied

Q2 Write a sentence in French like the one below about each of these pictures.

à Londres   ⟹   **Je vais à Londres en train.**

I am going to London on the train.

Look out — most types of transport need 'en', but one needs 'à'.

1) au collège

2) au terrain de sport

3) en ville

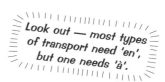

4) en Italie

5) au cinéma

Q3 Write out each French sentence a) to f) along with the matching English one from the box.

eg Je dois descendre à quel arrêt d'autobus? ⟹ **Which bus stop do I have to get out at?**

a) Je dois descendre à quel arrêt d'autobus?   d) À quelle heure arrive le bateau?

b) Est-ce que je peux apporter mon bébé?   e) Est-ce que je peux y aller en métro?

c) Quel train va à Lyon?   f) Quand part le bateau?

> **Which bus stop do I have to get out at?**   **When does the boat leave?**
>
> **Can I go there on the underground?**   **Can I bring my baby?**
>
> **What time does the boat arrive?**   **Which train is going to Lyon?**

Lost Property

Q1 Jeanne went on a day trip yesterday.
Read this passage about her trip and answer the questions below.

Une Excursion à Deauville

Hier, je faisais une petite excursion à Deauville par autobus. J'ai vu la cathédrale de Deauville, et j'ai fait quelques achats dans les magasins. Mais quand je suis sortie du bus, je n'avais plus mon sac!

Je sais que j'avais toujours mon sac quand je suis arrivée à la gare routière de Deauville. Je pense que j'ai pu laisser mon sac sur un banc dans la gare routière. Il n'y a pas d'argent dans mon sac. J'ai mis mon porte-monnaie dans la poche de ma veste. Mon sac est en cuir rouge, et il est assez petit.

Handy words:

une excursion = day trip	les achats = purchases
je n'avais plus = I no longer had	la gare routière = coach station
un banc = bench	le porte-monnaie = purse/wallet
en cuir = made of leather	la veste = jacket

a) Where did Jeanne go on her trip?

b) How did she travel there?

c) What tourist attraction did she see there?

d) What else did she do?

e) What happened when she left the bus?

f) Did Jeanne have it with her when she arrived at the station?

g) Where does she think she left it?

h) Was there any money in it?

i) Where did Jeanne put her purse?

j) What is Jeanne's bag made of?

k) What colour is it?

l) What size does she say it is?

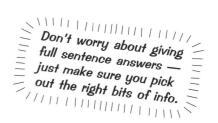
Don't worry about giving full sentence answers — just make sure you pick out the right bits of info.

School Subjects

Q1 Write out each English school subject name from the oval.
Put the matching French name next to each English one.

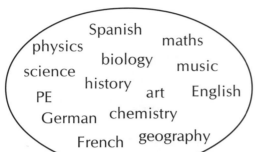

Spanish   maths

physics   biology   music

science   history

PE   art   English

German   chemistry

French   geography

la biologie   la chimie
l'éducation physique   l'espagnol
la géographie   l'anglais
le dessin   la physique
l'histoire   le français
la musique   les sciences
les mathématiques   l'allemand

Q2 Read this letter from Brigitte about the subjects she takes at school and
what she thinks of them. Then answer the true or false questions below.

Marseille, le 5 mai

Chère Lucy,

Merci de ta lettre. Comme toi, je n'aime pas toutes les
matières à l'école. En ce moment, je fais sept matières.

J'aime beaucoup les sciences — j'aime la biologie, mais ma
matière préférée est la chimie.

Je déteste le sport, parce que je ne suis pas très forte. J'aime
la géographie, mais je préfère les maths. Je fais de l'anglais et du
français aussi. Quelle est ta matière préférée?

Amitiés,

Brigitte

Écrivez **V** (vrai) ou **F** (faux) à côté de chaque phrase.

Exemple:

Brigitte fait de la géographie. | V | Brigitte n'aime pas le sport. | |

Brigitte fait de la biologie. | | Sa matière préférée est le français. | |

Brigitte fait du français. | | Elle préfère les maths à la géographie. | |

Brigitte aime les sciences. | | Brigitte fait de l'anglais. | |

School Routine

Q1   Write a full sentence in French saying how each person gets to school.

eg ***Jean-Luc (en voiture)*** ➡ ***Jean-Luc <u>va au collège</u> en voiture.***

Jean-Luc goes to college by car.

Jean-Luc (en voiture)   Anne-Marie (en bus)   François (à pied)

Louis (en train)   Eloise (en vélo)   Léon (en bus)

Etienne (en voiture)   Virginie (à pied)

Remember — you need 'en' with all transport <u>except</u> 'à pied' — on foot...

Q2   Read this passage about Jean-Luc's day and answer the questions below it in English.

<u>Le Jour au Collège</u>

À huit heures moins le quart, je vais au collège en autobus avec mes copains. Les cours commencent à huit heures. Nous avons huit cours par jour. Chaque cours dure quarante minutes.

À dix heures vingt, nous avons une pause de vingt minutes. À midi, nous avons la pause de midi.

Les cours finissent à quatorze heures trente-cinq. Nous faisons une heure de devoirs par jour.

<u>Useful words</u>:
les copains = friends   les cours = lessons
la pause = break   devoirs = homework

a)   What time does Jean-Luc go to school?

b)   How does he get to school?

c)   When do lessons begin?

d)   How many lessons are there per day?

e)   How long does each lesson last?

f)   What happens at 10:20am?

g)   When is the lunch break?

h)   What time do lessons finish?

i)   How much homework does he do every day?

School Stuff

Q1   Look at Ben's school timetable and answer the questions below it.

L'horaire de Ben:

	lundi	mardi	mercredi	jeudi	vendredi
9.00-9.40	Les maths	L'anglais	Les maths	Le français	La chimie
9.45-10.25	La physique	L'histoire	Les maths	La physique	La chimie
10.50-11.30	Le dessin	Le français	L'histoire	Les maths	Le français
11.35-12.15	L'anglais	Le français	La chimie	L'anglais	L'histoire
12.20-13.00	Le français	Les maths	L'anglais	L'anglais	Les maths
14.00-14.40	La chimie	La physique	Le français	La musique	Le dessin
14.45-15.25	La chimie	La physique	Le dessin	La musique	Le dessin

a)   Answer these questions in English.

   i)   What is Ben's first lesson on Tuesday? And on Thursday?

   ii) How many history lessons does he have each week?

   iii) How many chemistry lessons does he have on Friday?

   iv) How many double chemistry lessons does he have each week?

   v)   What lesson does Ben have last on Tuesday?

   vi) What is Ben's fourth lesson on Wednesday?

b)   Répondez à ces questions en français.

HINT: It's a whole lot easier if you use the words of the question to help you write the answer.

eg *À quelle heure finissent les cours?* ⇨ *Les cours finissent à...*
    Combien de temps dure chaque cours? ⇨ *Chaque cours dure...*

   i)   Quel est que le premier cours de Ben le mercredi?

   ii) À quelle heure commencent les cours?

   iii) À quelle heure finissent les cours?

   iv) Ben a combien de cours par jour?

   v)   Combien de temps dure chaque cours?

Make mine a double.

School Stuff

Q1 Look at these descriptions of two school uniforms and answer the questions in French.

<u>**Mike**</u>
Notre uniforme est un pullover rouge, un pantalon gris ou noir, une chemise blanche et une cravate verte.

<u>**Sarah**</u>
Au collège, notre uniforme est une veste bleue, une chemise grise ou blanche, une jupe ou un pantalon gris, et une cravate jaune et rouge.

a) Répondez à ces questions:

Le pullover de Mike est de quelle couleur?

Qui doit porter une veste bleue?

La cravate de Sarah est de quelle couleur?

Qui doit porter une cravate verte?

Est-ce que Mike peut porter un pantalon rouge?

Est-ce que Sarah peut porter une jupe?

> *Helpful words:*
> un pullover = jumper
> un pantalon = trousers
> une chemise = shirt
> une cravate = tie
> une veste = jacket
> une jupe = skirt

Don't worry about answering in full sentences but remember to give your answers in French.

Q2 Read this passage and answer the true or false questions.

No really, banana studies.

> À huit heures je prends le petit déjeuner. Je vais à l'école à pied. Les cours commencent à huit heures quarante-cinq. Nous avons huit cours par jour.
> Ma matière préférée est le français. À dix heures et demie nous avons la récréation, puis à une heure nous avons la pause du déjeuner. Les cours finissent à trois heures et demie.

Écrivez **V** (vrai) ou **F** (faux):

Il va à l'école à pied. **V**	Ils ont neuf cours par jour. ☐
Sa matière préférée est l'anglais. ☐	Les cours commencent à huit heures. ☐
Les cours finissent à trois heures. ☐	Ils ont le déjeuner à une heure. ☐

Use the vocab on the last couple of pages to help you.

Types of Jobs

Q1   Write out the French job words a) to w) and pick the matching English words from the box.

a) le/la comptable

b) le/la secrétaire

c) l'ingénieur

d) le/la mécanicien(ne)

e) l'électricien(ne)

f) le plombier

g) le/la chef de cuisine

h) le boulanger / la boulangère

i) l'acteur / l'actrice

j) le/la musicien(ne)

k) le vendeur / la vendeuse

l) le/la journaliste

m) le/la prof(esseur)

n) le coiffeur / la coiffeuse

o) le gendarme / la femme policier

p) le facteur / la factrice

q) l'agent immobilier (masc.)

r) le/la dentiste

s) le/la pharmacien(ne)

t) l'infirmier / l'infirmière

u) le médecin

v) l'étudiant(e)

w) le boucher / la bouchère

---

actor   secretary   doctor   engineer   butcher   plumber   chemist

musician   salesperson   chef   journalist   dentist   hairdresser   mechanic   nurse

student   electrician

policeman/woman   estate agent   accountant   baker   postman/woman   teacher

---

Q2   You're looking for a job in France to improve your French. Read these job adverts and answer the questions in English.

Ⓐ
SI VOUS CHERCHEZ
UN JOB POUR LES VACANCES
adressez-vous à
CAMÉO VIDÉO
562.43.22
16, Rue de la Mer
Nous cherchons un(e) assistant(e)

Ⓑ

Élégant et raffiné
Salon de thé
*Cherche
serveur/serveuse
Immédiatement*
33 Avenue de la plage
BÉNODET — 67 41 08 92

Ⓒ
confiserie
CHERCHE
VENDEUSE
Quatre heures par jour,
du lundi au vendredi
485.62.78

a) What kind of job is being advertised in advert 'A'? Can both males and females apply for it?

b) What job is being advertised in advert 'B'?

c) Could both men and women apply?

d) When is the job for?

e) What kind of place is advertising in advert 'C'?

f) What do they want?

g) What are the hours of the job?

More Jobs

Q1 Read this letter from Anne-Laure talking about her parents' jobs and what job she'd like to do in the future. Answer the questions below in English.

> Paris, le 10 janvier
>
> Salut!
>
> Je suis très contente d'avoir un(e) correspondant(e) britannique. J'ai quinze ans et j'habite un grand appartement avec ma famille à Paris. Ma mère est plombier et mon père est ingénieur. Ma mère aime être plombier, parce qu'elle a le sens pratique.
>
> Mon père n'aime pas beaucoup son travail. Il doit travailler cinquante heures par semaine et c'est trop pour lui. Il n'est pas satisfait de son emploi.
>
> Je pense que je voudrais devenir femme policier parce que j'adore le danger et l'uniforme. Que font tes père et mère dans la vie? Qu'est-ce que tu voudrais devenir plus tard et pourquoi?
>
> Amitiés
>
> Anne-Laure

You don't have to understand every word — just pick out what you need.

a) What does Anne-Laure say in her first sentence?

b) What job does she say her mother does?

c) What job does she say her father does?

d) Does her mother like her job? Why?/Why not?

e) Does her father like his job? Why?/Why not?

f) What job does Anne-Laure want?

g) Why does she want to do that job?

Q2 This question's all about saying what you'd like to become in the future and why. Write sentences in French, like the example below, for each job a) and b).

> eg *chef de cusine — j'adore préparer les repas*
>
> ⟹ *__Je voudrais devenir__ chef de cuisine, __parce que__ j'adore préparer les repas.*
>
> I would like to become a chef, because I love to prepare meals.

a) mécanicien(ne) — je m'intéresse aux voitures

b) coiffeur/coiffeuse — la mode me plaît

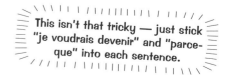

This isn't that tricky — just stick "je voudrais devenir" and "parce-que" into each sentence.

Sports

Q1 Here's a couple of ads for French sports centres.
Use them to answer the questions below in English.

Piscine de Lyon

adultes €2
enfants €1,25

Heures d'ouverture

du lundi au vendredi :
de 7h00 à 13h00 et de 14h30 à 21h00
samedi et dimanche :
de 7h00 à 19h00 sans interruption.
réservé aux dames
mardi et mercredi : de 16h00 à 18h00

aérobic en piscine   lundi et jeudi
14h30 à 15h30 (avancé)
dimanche 10h00 à 11h30 (novice)

gymnase   du lundi au vendredi :
de 11h00 à 13h00 et de 14h30 à 19h00
samedi et dimanche :
de 11h00 à 18h00 sans interruption.

rafraîchissements

Sports à l'école
St. Christophe

volley-ball
basket
tennis de table
badminton

du lundi au vendredi :
de 18h00 à 22h00
samedi et dimanche :
de 10h30 à 15h00

€1/€0,5 moins de 15 ans

Read the information really carefully so you don't slip up.

a) Can you go swimming at 3pm on Wednesday afternoon?

b) Where can you play table tennis after 10.30 am on a Saturday?

c) What time is the pool aerobics class on Thursday?

   A between 2.30 and 3.30 pm   **B** between 10.00 and 11.30 am

d) When is the swimming pool reserved for women?

   A Monday and Wednesday from 4-6 pm   **B** Tuesday and Wednesday from 4-6 pm

e) How much does it cost for an adult to go swimming?

f) How much does it cost for someone under 15 to use St Christophe's school?

g) Can you play tennis at St. Christophe's school?

h) At which of the sports centres could you buy something to eat or drink?

   A Piscine de Lyon   **B** l'école St Christophe

Hobbies

Q1 Pick the right French name from the box for each instrument below and write it out.

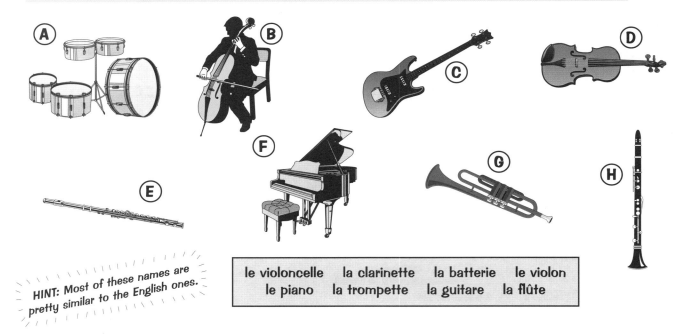

HINT: Most of these names are pretty similar to the English ones.

| le violoncelle | la clarinette | la batterie | le violon |
| le piano | la trompette | la guitare | la flûte |

Q2 Write out this passage in French, filling in each gap with the right phrase from the box.

Célia adore le sport. Elle a un nouveau vélo et elle .... Elle porte ....
en lycra et un casque de cyclisme .... pour .... Quand il pleut, Célia
joue en général au squash ou au .... avec son amie Ghislaine.

Read it all and work out what it means first — then fill in the gaps so it makes sense.

violet   un short rose   tennis de table
fait souvent du cyclisme   sa propre sécurité

Q3 This is all about saying what you think of something in French and why.
Write down answers to each question in full French sentences.

eg Qu'est-ce que tu penses du football?

→ _J'aime beaucoup le football parce que j'aime faire de l'exercice._

a) Qu'est-ce que tu penses d'aller à la pêche?

b) Qu'est-ce que tu penses de la musique classique?

c) Qu'est-ce que tu penses de la musique rock?

Remember: parce que = because

Sports & Hobbies

Q1 Read these interviews with four French kids about what sports they play. Pick the right answer for each question, **A**, **B** or **C**.

It looks boring — but it's dead easy. Read the questions first then look for the right bits in the French.

Françoise: Est-ce que tu fais du sport?
Chantelle: Oui, je joue au football le week-end.
Françoise: Tu joues avec qui?
Chantelle: Je joue avec beaucoup de mes amis.
Françoise: Tu aimes jouer au football?
Chantelle: Mais oui, il est très amusant de jouer au football.

* * * * * * * * * * * * * * * * *

Françoise: Est-ce que tu fais du sport?
Jacques: Oui, je joue au hockey.
Françoise: Qu-est-ce que tu penses du hockey?
Jacques: J'aime le hockey, parce que c'est un sport passionnant.

passionnant = exciting

Françoise: Est-ce que tu fais du sport?
Xavier: Oui, je joue au squash le mardi.
Françoise: Tu joues au squash où et avec qui?
Xavier: Je joue dans le centre sportif à l'école. Je joue avec mon ami Stéphane. Nous sommes membres d'un club de squash.

* * * * * * * * * * * * * * * * *

Françoise: Est-ce que tu fais du sport?
Sophie: Oui, je vais nager le mercredi et le samedi.
Françoise: Tu vas nager avec qui?
Sophie: Le mercredi je nage avec un club de natation et le samedi je nage avec ma famille.

a) Who likes to go swimming?

   A Jacques   **B** Chantelle   **C** Sophie

b) When do they swim?

   A Tuesday and Saturday   **B** Wednesday and Friday   **C** Wednesday and Saturday

c) Who thinks the sport they play is exciting?

   A Jacques   **B** Sophie   **C** Xavier

d) Who plays their sport at the weekend?

   A Xavier   **B** Chantelle   **C** No one

There's only one right answer for each question.

e) Who does Chantelle play football with?

   A her mum   **B** Manchester United   **C** her friends

f) Who does their sport with their family?

   A Jacques   **B** Chantelle   **C** Sophie

g) What does Chantelle think of football?

   A it's boring   **B** it's difficult   **C** it's fun

Going Out

Q1 Write out each of these French words a) to f) with the matching English word from the box.

a) le spectacle

b) le film

c) le billet

d) un billet à prix reduit

e) commence

f) finit

a reduced-price ticket
starts
the film
finishes
the ticket
performance

Q2 Look at this advert and answer the questions in English.

_This is easy if you know your
days of the week in French._

a) How much does a full-price ticket cost?

b) How much does a reduced-price ticket cost?

c) Can you watch 'La Haine' on Saturday?

d) What time does 'Astérix et Obélix' start on Saturday?

e) What time does the film 'La Haine' start on Sunday?

f) Is the cinema open every day?

CINÉMA ROXY

lundi, mardi et **vendredi**
La Haine : 19h00; 22h30
samedi
Astérix et Obélix : 12h00
Les Convoyeurs en Attendant :
14h00; 18h00; 21h00
dimanche :
Astérix et Obélix :
12h00; 14h30
Les Convoyeurs en Attendant :
18h00; 21h00
La Haine : 22h30

BILLET : €5/€3

Q3 Read what your new French friend, Laurent, has to say about the cinema and answer the questions below.

LAURENT DIT: **Moi, j'aime aller au cinéma. J'y vais tous les mois.
Je regarde au moins un nouveau film chaque mois.*
Mes films préférés sont les films d'action mais j'adore
aussi tous les films étrangers.**

a) How often does Laurent see new films?   c) What other kind of films does he like?

b) What is his favourite kind of film?

*au moins = at least

Inviting People Out or Staying In

Q1   In this question practice saying "Let's go..." in French.
Turn each English sentence below into French and write it out nicely.

> *eg Let's go to the swimming pool.* ➡ <u>*Allons*</u> *à la piscine.*

Let's go = Allons

Allons nager!

a)   Let's go to the park. ➡ .... *au parc.*

b)   Let's go to the theatre. ➡ .... *au théâtre.*

c)   Let's go to the cinema. ➡ .... *au cinéma.*

d)   Let's go to a concert. ➡ .... *au concert.*

e)   Let's go swimming. ➡ .... *nager.*

f)   Let's go dancing. ➡ .... *danser.*

Q2   This question's all about arranging to meet someone.
Turn each English sentence a) to f) into French and write it out.

Use this example to help you:

On se retrouve = We'll meet

We'll meet in front of the town hall at 2pm.

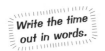
Write the time out in words.

➡ *On se retrouve devant la mairie à deux heures.*

a)   We'll meet in front of the cinema at 7pm.   ➡ *...devant le cinéma à ...*

b)   We'll meet inside the disco at 9.30pm.   ➡ *...dans la discothèque à ...*

c)   We'll meet next to the sports centre at 11am.   ➡ *...à côté du centre sportif à ...*

d)   We'll meet at the bus stop at 4:15pm.   ➡ *...à l'arrêt d'autobus à ...*

e)   We'll meet at your house at 6pm.   ➡ *...chez toi à ...*

f)   We'll meet at the park at 8:45pm.   ➡ *...au parc à ...*

Favourite Entertainments

Q1 Chantelle and Henri are banging on in French about what they like to do for fun. All you need to do is pick the right answer **A**, **B** or **C** for the questions underneath.

> Ma vraie passion, c'est le cinéma. Mes copines et moi, on sort presque toutes les semaines pour voir un film. Mes films préférés? Les films policiers me plaisent, mais j'ai vu récemment un film comique qui était sensass.

Chantelle

> Le cinéma? Ça va, mais je préfère regarder la télé chez moi. J'adore l'émission 'Hélène et les garçons', mais j'aime aussi regarder les actualités.

Henri

a) What is Chantelle's passion?

A cinema **B** music **C** comedians

b) How often does she go to the cinema with her friends?

A every other week **B** every week **C** twice a week

c) What sort of film did she see recently?

A a thriller **B** a comedy **C** an adventure film

d) What does Henri prefer to do?

A read books **B** listen to the radio **C** watch television

e) What type of programme does he like apart from 'Hélène et les garçons'?

A the news **B** soap operas **C** documentaries

Q2 These questions are about what you like. Write full French sentences to answer them. Use the stuff from Q1 for ideas.

eg *Est-ce que tu aimes le football?* ➡ *Je trouve le football ennuyeux.*

Do you like football?   I find football boring.

a) Qu'est-ce que tu aimes regarder à la télévision? ➡ *J'aime regarder ...*

b) Est-ce que tu as un film préféré? ➡ *Oui, mon film préféré est ...*

c) Qu'est-ce que tu penses de la musique? ➡ *Je trouve la musique ...*

Times and Opening Hours

Q1 Pick the right French time from the box for each clock **A** to **H**.

eg **A:** *Il est neuf heures et quart.*

 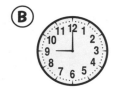  

   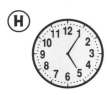

WHAT TIME IS IT?

Il est quatre heures moins vingt.   *Il est cinq heures cinq.*

Il est treize heures dix.   *Il est huit heures moins vingt-cinq.*

Il est dix heures cinquante-cinq.   *Il est dix heures moins le quart.*

Il est neuf heures et quart.   *Il est neuf heures.*

Q2 Pick the TWO right ways of saying the time in French on each clock 1 to 6 below.
Remember — for each clock there are TWO right ways and ONE wrong one.

*Don't forget — some of the French
bits will be from the 24-hour clock.*

eg

   ⓐ Il est onze heures moins
vingt-cinq.

   ⓑ Il est vingt-deux heures
trente-cinq.

   c) Il est dix heures vingt-cinq.

a) Il est cinq heures moins vingt-cinq.

b) Il est cinq heures moins trente-cinq.

c) Il est seize heures trente-cinq.

a) Il est deux heures vingt-cinq.

b) Il est quatorze heures vingt.

c) Il est deux heures vingt.

a) Il est treize heures.

b) Il est quinze heures.

c) Il est trois heures.

a) Il est midi.

b) Il est minuit.

c) Il est midi heures.

a) Il est deux heures moins dix.

b) Il est treize heures cinquante.

c) Il est treize heures dix.

Times and Appointments

Q1   Imagine it's the 12th of October today. Here's your calendar in French showing everything you'll be doing in October. Read it and answer the questions below in English.

octobre

DIMANCHE	LUNDI	MARDI	MERCREDI	JEUDI	VENDREDI	SAMEDI
		1	**2** 18h30: aller nager avec Pierrick, Hermine et Guy. Piscine.	**3**	**4** Finir projet de géographie!!!	**5** 10h45: Vétérinaire avec Dodo qui a mal à la jambe.
6 13h30: Jeu de basket avec ma famille. Stade sportif.	**7**	**8** 19h30:cinéma avec Hermine, Phébé, Arnaud & Guy - 'La Femme Nikita'	**9**	**10** 15h15 rendez-vous chez le dentiste	**11**	**12** 11h40 rendez-vous chez la coiffeuse
13 12h15 Baptême de mon neveu, Juste à L'église St Marie.	**14** 19h45: Théâtre avec Pierrick, Aurélie et Yves.	**15**	**16** 15h30: entraînement de hockey avec l'équipe de hockey	**17**	**18** 18h00 faire du shopping avec ma mère	**19**
20 14h00: Jouer au tennis avec Hermine - centre sportif	**21**	**22** 20h30 Jouer au bowling avec Pierrick, Guy, Fleur, Yves et Iris.	**23** 16h00: match de hockey *crosse de hockey	**24**	**25** 21h15: Disco! Avec Aurélie et Hermine.	**26**
27 14h00: Visite chez mes grands-parents. Grenoble.	**28** 20h00: Restaurant avec Pierrick.	**29**	**30** 20h00: vidéo chez moi avec Pierrick et Hermine.	**31**		

a) What are you doing this morning?

b) What are you doing on the 14th?

c) What are you doing on the 16th? What time are you doing it?

d) What date are you going to watch a video?

e) Who are you going to the disco with on Friday the 25th?

f) What are you going to do on Tuesday 22nd October?

g) Where are you visiting your grandparents on the 27th?

h) What piece of equipment musn't you forget on Wednesday 23rd October?

i) What date did you go swimming and at what time?

j) What date did you have to finish your geography project on?

k) What film did you watch last Tuesday? What time did you watch it?

*crosse de hockey = hockey stick

Remember — work out the dates for the answers as though *today* is the *12th October*.

Shopping

Q1   Here's a load of useful stuff for talking about shopping in French. Write out each French phrase a) to h) along with the matching English one from the circle.

_eg_ _Je voudrais un kilo de sucre, s'il vous plaît._ ⟹ _I would like a kilo of sugar, please._

a)   "Je voudrais un kilo de sucre, s'il vous plaît."

b)   "Celui-ci ou celui-là?"

c)   "Je le prends."

d)   "Ça coûte combien?"

e)   "Des grandes ou des petites?"

f)   "Autre chose?"

g)   "C'est tout?"

h)   "Ça coûte huit euros cinquante."

Anything else?

I'll take it.

I would like a kilo of sugar, please.

That costs 8 euros 50.

This one or that one?

How much is it?

Big ones or small ones?

Will that be all?

Q2   Look at this conversation at the grocer's. Write the whole thing out in French turning all the English bits into French as well. Use Q1 and the vocab to help you.

GROCER'S

VOUS: Excuse me, do you have sugar?

L'ÉPICIÈRE: Bien sûr. Combien de grammes voudriez-vous?

VOUS: 500g please. Do you have any tea?

L'ÉPICIÈRE: Oui. Du thé anglais ou du thé au citron?

VOUS: How much is the lemon tea?

L'ÉPICIÈRE: Ce paquet coûte deux euros.

VOUS: I'll take it.

Tricky vocab
do you have any...
   = avez-vous..
tea = du thé
sugar = du sucre
500 = cinq cent
lemon = citron

Shopping for Clothes

Q1   Turn these French sentences into English ones.

eg Je porte une chemise blanche. ⟹ I'm wearing a white shirt.

Hot stuff...

a) Je porte des chaussures noires.

b) Laurent porte un imperméable rouge.

c) Sylvie aime les jupes blanches.

d) En hiver, je porte des gants bruns.

e) Ma cravate est verte.

f) Mon frère a une veste blanche.

Use the vocab box at the bottom of the page to help.

Q2   Write down the French name and colour of each of these bits of clothing.

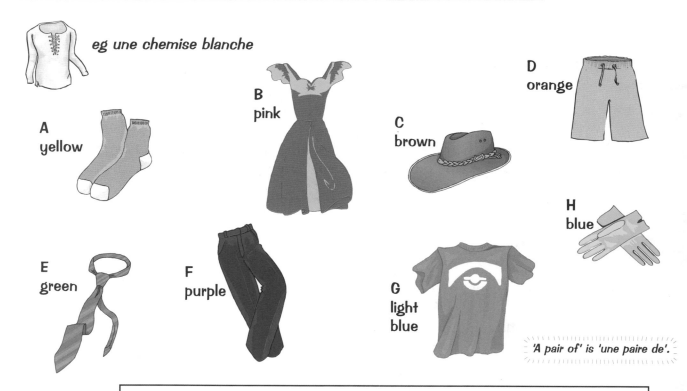

eg une chemise blanche

B pink

D orange

A yellow

C brown

H blue

E green

F purple

G light blue

'A pair of' is 'une paire de'.

You might as well learn this list — it'll come in dead handy.

Useful Vocab

les chaussettes	*socks*	le short	*shorts*
la cravate	*tie*	les gants	*gloves*
le pantalon	*trousers*	l'imperméable	*waterproof*
la robe	*dress*	la jupe	*skirt*
le chapeau	*hat*	la veste	*waistcoat*
le T-shirt	*T-shirt*	le manteau	*coat*
		la chemise	*shirt*

More Shopping

Q1 This table shows how much pocket money three French teenagers get
and what they spend it on. Answer the questions underneath in English.

Nom	Combien d'argent de poche	Ce qu'il/elle achète
Véronique	**€4 par semaine**	**Vêtements, des CD**
Gérard	**€7 tous les quinze jours**	**Livres, bonbons**
Sandrine	**€4,5 par semaine**	**Jeux, magazines**

a) How much pocket money does Véronique get each week?

b) Does Gérard get pocket money every week?

c) What does Sandrine buy with her pocket money?

d) Who likes reading?

e) Who likes listening to music?

Give your answer in English.

Q2 Read these adverts for sales and price cuts, and answer the questions in English.

Librairie Michel Lèsne
SOLDES!
Tout est à prix réduit!
Dépêchez-vous — les soldes
durent jusqu'au 12 OCT.

Grand magasin 'Galeries'
SOLDES DU PRINTEMPS
Pull-overs,
manteaux,
gants, chapeaux
sont tous à moitié prix

a) What can you buy at Michel Lèsne's shop?

b) How much in the shop is being sold at a reduced price?

c) When does the sale end?

d) How much is the CD player reduced by?

e) What time of year is the sale at the Galeries?

f) What kind of clothes are being sold off cheap?

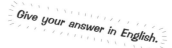

Réduction de 25%

> **_Tricky vocab_**
> *la librairie = bookshop*
> *le printemps = spring*

Food

Q1 Turn these two fun-packed shopping lists into English using the words from the box below.

It's best to do the easy ones first.

Liste d'achats

petits pains	haricots verts
yaourts	une salade
céréales	oignons
lait	pêches
oeufs	framboises
carottes	sel
champignons	fromage

Supermarché

pommes de terre	pommes frites
un concombre	bifteck
un chou	poulet
tomates	café
pommes et bananes	thé
un citron	confiture de fraises
petits pois	jambon
	glace à la vanille
	jus d'orange

meuh

beef	a cucumber	apples and bananas
tomatoes	mushrooms	coffee
a lemon	chicken	raspberries
carrots	eggs	a lettuce
ham	green beans	peas
onions	potatoes	bread rolls
yogurts	cereals	tea
peaches	salt	milk
strawberry jam	vanilla ice cream	cheese
a cauliflower	chips	orange juice

Q2 Imagine you're in a nice French café which serves typical French grub.
Turn this menu into English and write it out for your annoying little brother.

Casse-croûtes*	**À boire**
croque-monsieur	citron pressé
(pain grillé, fromage et jambon)	_(jus de citron frais, eau, sucre)_
croque-madame	thé, café
(pain grillé, fromage et un oeuf)	jus d'orange
croissants	**Hors d'oeuvre**
(avec beurre et confiture)	crudités
	escargots

Handy vocab

grillé = toasted
crudités = raw vegetables
escargots = snails

*snacks

Meals

Q1 Write out each of the French sentences below along with the matching English one.

eg Pouvez-vous me passer le poivre, s'il vous plaît? ⟹ *Could you pass me the pepper, please?*

Pouvez-vous me passer le poivre, s'il vous plaît?

Est-ce que je pourrais avoir une serviette?

Voudrais-tu du bifteck?

J'ai assez mangé, merci.

Je voudrais beaucoup de fromage, s'il vous plaît.

Ça suffit.

Voudriez-vous une grande portion de crêpes?

Would you like a large portion of pancakes?

That's enough.

I would like a lot of cheese, please.

Could I have a napkin?

Could you pass me the pepper, please?

Would you like some steak?

I've eaten enough, thank you.

Q2 Lucky you — you're having a meal at a French family's house. During the evening meal, they ask you these questions 1) to 6) below. Write down what each one means.

1) Est-ce que tu as faim?

2) Qu'est-ce que tu aimes manger?

3) As-tu soif?

4) Est-ce que tu voudrais encore quelque chose?

5) Aimes-tu l'agneau?

6) Tu préfères le thé ou le café?

Handy words

soif = thirsty   faim = hungry
manger = to eat   l'agneau = lamb

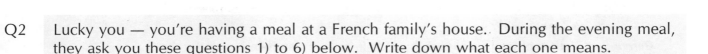

Why do English people have two eggs for breakfast, and French people only have one?

Because 'un oeuf' is enough...

Q3 The meal's over. Write out each English sentence a) to c) along with the matching French one, 1) to 3).

a) I've eaten enough, thanks.

b) The meal was delicious.

c) I liked the dinner.

1) Le dîner m'a plu.

2) J'ai assez mangé, merci.

3) Le repas était délicieux.

Restaurant

Q1   Read this French conversation in a restaurant and answer the questions about it in English.

Read it all through first, then come back to any bits you don't understand.

Garçon: Bonsoir, madame, monsieur. Vous voudriez une table pour deux personnes?

Isabelle: Oui, c'est ça, merci.

Claude: Est-ce que nous pouvons nous asseoir sur la terrasse?

Garçon: Mais certainement, monsieur.

Claude (plus tard):   Garçon! Est-ce que nous pourrions voir la carte, s'il vous plaît?

Garçon: Oui, monsieur. Vous voudriez commander quelque chose à boire?

Isabelle: Moi, je voudrais un vin rouge.

Claude: Pour moi, de l'eau minérale, s'il vous plaît.

Isabelle: Qu'est-ce que c'est le plat du jour?

Garçon: C'est du canard rôti avec de la sauce à l'orange.

Claude: Et c'est comment?

Garçon: C'est très très bon — c'est une spécialité de la maison.

Claude: Est-ce que vous avez des crudités?

Garçon: Oui — est-ce que vous en voudriez?

Claude: Oui, une portion de crudités s'il vous plaît, et pour le plat principal, la truite avec des pommes frites et des légumes.

Isabelle: Et pour moi une omelette aux champignons. Où sont les toilettes, s'il vous plaît?

Garçon: Vous montez l'escalier au bout de la salle, et les toilettes sont à droite.

Isabelle (plus tard):   Est-ce que nous pouvons payer?

Garçon: Certainement, madame.

Use the words in the 'Vital Vocab' box to help.

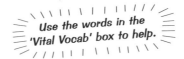

a)   What time of day is it — morning or evening?

b)   How can you tell?

c)   Where do Claude and Isabelle want to sit?

d)   What does Claude ask for after they have sat down?

e)   Who orders a mineral water?

f)   Does Isabelle want red or white wine?

g)   What item on the menu does Isabelle ask about?

h)   What kind of sauce comes with the roast duck?

i)   What does Claude have as a starter?

j)   What does Isabelle order?

k)   What is the last thing the pair ask if they can do?

Vital Vocab

sur la terrasse
      = on the terrace
plus tard = later
la carte = menu
le plat du jour
      = dish of the day
canard rôti = roast duck
truite = trout
Bonsoir = Good evening
payer = pay
l'escalier = staircase

Restaurant

Q1   Pick the right French way to say each of these English phrases. Write out the French one.

we'd like a table for four
> nous voudrions nous asseoir quatre fois
> nous voudrions quatre tables
> nous voudrions une table pour quatre personnes

> je ne suis plus satisfait(e)
> je ne suis pas satisfait(e)  **I'm not satisfied**
> je ne suis pas satisfié(e)

we'd like to sit outside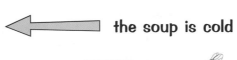
> nous voudrions asseoir à l'extérieur
> nous voudrions nous asseoir à l'extérieur
> nous voudrions nous asseoir à l'intérieur

> le potage est froid
> le potage a froid 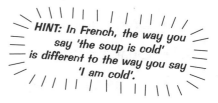 **the soup is cold**
> le potage est chaud

> *HINT: In French, the way you say 'the soup is cold' is different to the way you say 'I am cold'.*

Q2   Here's another restaurant conversation. Write it out in French, turning all the bits in English into French. Use the menu and the stuff on the last two pages to help you.

SERVEUSE: Bonsoir mesdames, messieurs.

VOUS: I'd like a table for four, please.

SERVEUSE: Voudriez-vous quelque chose à boire?

VOUS: Yes, one mineral water and three glasses of white wine.

SERVEUSE: Du pain avec ça?

VOUS: Yes please.

SERVEUSE (plus tard): Êtes-vous prêts à commander?

VOUS: Yes. To start with, two omelettes, one salad and one soup. Then the roast chicken for two and the seafood for two.

SERVEUSE: Qu'est-ce que vous voudriez comme légumes?

VOUS: Do you have carrots and potatoes?

SERVEUSE: Oui, nous en avons.

VOUS: Two portions of potatoes au gratin and two of rice, and carrots for everyone please.

Hors d'oeuvre
Omelette espagnole (spanish omelette)
Salade (salad)
Potage du jour (soup of the day)

Plat principal
Poulet rôti (roast chicken)
Boeuf Bourguignon (beef bourguignon)
Fruits de mer mixtes (mixed seafood)

Carottes à la Vichy (vichy carrots)
Pommes de terre au gratin (potatoes in a cream sauce)
Riz (rice)

Desserts
Glace au chocolat (chocolate ice cream)
Fruits divers (assorted fruits)

Café (coffee)
Fromage (cheese)

Your Family

Q1 An easy one to start the page off — write down who all these relatives are in English.

    a) La mère   c) Le grand-père   e) La soeur   g) La grand-mère   i) La cousine

    b) Le cousin   d) La tante   f) Le père   h) L'oncle   j) Le frère

Q2 Your French penfriend has asked you some questions. Write down your answers in French.

For some of the questions, I've written in the <u>start</u> of your answer sentence to help.

- Tu es grand(e) ou petit(e)?   **Je suis...**

- De quelle couleur sont tes cheveux?   **Mes cheveux sont...**

- Est-ce que tes cheveux sont raides ou frisés, courts ou longs?   **Mes cheveux sont...**

- De quelle couleur sont tes yeux?   **Mes yeux sont...**

- Quand est ton anniversaire?   **Mon anniversaire est le...**

- Il y a combien de personnes dans ta famille?   **Il y a ... personnes dans ma famille.**

- Tu as des animaux domestiques?

- Quel âge as-tu?   **J'ai ... ans.**

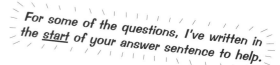

J'ai les cheveux bruns, et les yeux verts. Je ne sors pas très souvent...

Q3 Look at the animals a) to i) and pick the right French name for each one from the box. Write the names out.

Le chat

L'oiseau

Le cochon d'Inde

Le lapin

Le chien

La souris

Le cheval

Le poisson rouge

Le mouton

Where You Live

Q1 Look at the piccie of these houses and answer the questions in French about who lives where.

Give your answers using <u>your</u> left and right.

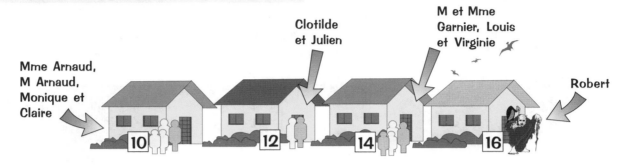

a) Monique habite à quel numéro?

b) Qui habite à côté de la famille Arnaud?

c) Robert a combien de voisins?*

d) Qui habite à la droite de Julien?

e) Qui habite au numéro dix?

f) Qui habite au numéro douze?

les voisins = neighbours

Q2 Look at this pic and answer the questions about who lives where. Answer in French.

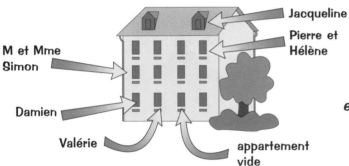

Remember to use 'habite' if you're talking about one person and 'habitent' if there are two or more.

eg Qui <u>habite</u> au premier étage?

Who lives on the first floor?

M et Mme Simon <u>habitent</u> au premier étage.

Mr and Mrs Simon live on the first floor.

Tricky Words

dans une mansarde = in an attic room
monter l'escalier = climb the stairs
les voisins = neighbours
étage = floor
rez-de-chaussée = ground floor

a) Qui habite au rez-de-chaussée?

b) Qui habite dans une mansarde?

c) Qui habite sous M et Mme Simon?

d) Qui doit monter l'escalier pour arriver à leur appartement?

There's no place like Rome.

Inside Your House

Q1 Here's a list of 6 things you might find in a bedroom. Pick the right French word for each of them from the box below and write them out.

a) bed   c) wardrobe   e) lamp
b) curtains   d) shelf   f) double bed

La lampe	Le grand lit
L'étagère	Les rideaux
Le lit	L'armoire

Q2 This is all about what furniture you've got in different rooms.
Write a full sentence answer in French for each question a) to d).
Use the pictures underneath to help you remember the furniture names.

eg *Quels meubles est-ce qu'il y a dans l'entrée?*

What bits of furniture are there in the entrance?

➡ *Dans l'entrée, il y a une lampe et un tapis.*

In the entrance, there's a lamp and a carpet.

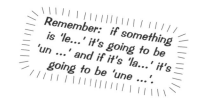

Remember: if something is 'le...' it's going to be 'un ...' and if it's 'la...' it's going to be 'une ...'.

a) Quels meubles est-ce qu'il y a dans le salon?

b) Quels meubles est-ce qu'il y a dans la salle de bains?

c) Quels meubles est-ce qu'il y a dans la salle à manger?

d) Quels meubles est-ce qu'il y a dans la cuisine?

le tapis

la table

la lampe

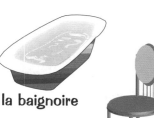
la baignoire

la chaise

le miroir

le fauteuil

la cuisinière

le placard

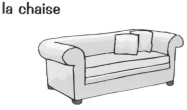
le canapé

Household Chores

Q1 Write out each of the French phrases about chores a) to i)
along with the matching English phrase from the box.

eg ranger ma chambre ➡ *tidy my room*

a) **ranger ma chambre**

b) **faire la vaisselle**

c) **passer l'aspirateur**

d) **faire mon lit**

e) **débarrasser la table**

f) **mettre la table**

g) **nettoyer la maison**

h) **préparer le dîner**

i) **laver les vêtements**

lay the table
do the washing up
make my bed
tidy my room
cook the supper
wash the clothes
clean the house
vacuum
clear the table

It's best just to learn these set phrases.

For a small dog, Toby was exceptionally gifted
when it came to clearing tables.

Q2 Rewrite these sentences so that instead of saying you <u>do</u> something,
you're saying you <u>have to</u> do something. Here's an example.

eg Je <u>passe</u> l'aspirateur. (passer) ➡ *Je <u>dois passer</u> l'aspirateur. * *

je dois = I have to

I do the vacuuming.   I have to do the vacuuming.

a) Je <u>fais</u> mon lit. (faire)

b) Je <u>fais</u> la vaisselle. (faire)

c) Je <u>lave</u> mes vêtements. (laver)

d) Je <u>range</u> ma chambre. (ranger)

e) Je <u>prépare</u> le dîner. (préparer)

f) Je <u>mets</u> la table. (mettre)

Q3 Put these French sentences into English.

Use the phrases from Q1 to help you.

eg   Je passe l'aspirateur. ➡ *I do the vacuuming.*

a) Je passe l'aspirateur.

b) Je prépare le déjeuner.

c) Je mets la table.

d) Je débarrasse la table.

e) Je range la chambre.

f) Je nettoie la salle de bains.

g) Je fais mon lit.

h) Je fais la vaisselle.

Parts of the Body

Q1 Pick the right French word from the box for each body part **A** to **J** on the picture.

eg A: le cou

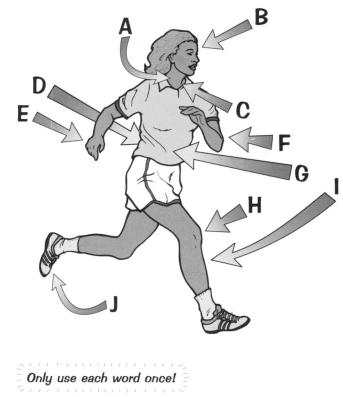

This topic is most likely to come up in the listening or speaking exam — so practise saying the words, too.

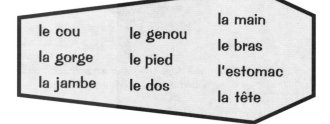

le cou	le genou	la main
la gorge	le pied	le bras
la jambe	le dos	l'estomac
		la tête

Only use each word once!

Q2 In these pictures, imagine the crosses show where each person's hurt. Pick the right French phrase from the box for each picture **A** to **F**.

eg A: J'ai mal à l'estomac.

I've got stomach ache.

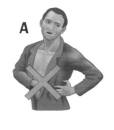 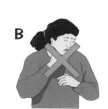 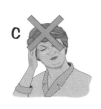   

| Mon doigt me fait mal. | J'ai mal à la gorge. | Mes mains me font mal. |
| J'ai mal à la tête. | Mon dos me fait mal. | J'ai mal à l'estomac. |

Telephones

Q1 Here are some questions about phone numbers — answer 'em in French sentences.

Jacques
96 05 22 81

Francine
41 82 35 47

Clotilde
20 99 50 09

Pizzaville
82 32 82 32

Phone numbers go in twos. So 41 56 37 60 = quarante et un, cinquante-six, trente-sept, soixante.

eg _Quel est le numéro de téléphone de Jacques?_

What is Jacques' phone number?

⟹ _Le numéro de téléphone de Jacques est le quatre-vingt-seize, zéro cinq, vingt deux, quatre-vingt-un._

a) Quel est le numéro de téléphone de Francine?
b) Quel est le numéro de téléphone de Clotilde?
c) Quel est le numéro de téléphone de Pizzaville?
d) Quel est ton numéro de téléphone?

Q2 Read this French conversation and answer the questions a) to f).

Anne André: Bonjour Madame Laurent. C'est Anne à l'appareil. Est-ce que je peux parler à Étienne, s'il vous plaît?
Mme Laurent: Ah — il est sorti tout à l'heure. Je suis désolée.
Anne André: Alors, est-ce que vous pouvez lui donner un message?
Mme Laurent: Mais bien sûr.
Anne André: Je voudrais lui demander s'il voudrait aller au cinéma demain soir avec Philippe et moi. Nous allons voir 'Les moutons enragés'.
Mme Laurent: Très bien. Je lui demanderai de vous rappeler demain matin — ça va?
Anne André: Ça sera parfait. Merci, Mme Laurent. Au revoir.

a) What French phrase does Anne use to say who she is?
b) Who does she want to speak to?
c) Why can't she speak to him?
d) What does Mme Laurent suggest instead?
e) When is Anne going to the cinema?
f) What will Mme Laurent ask Étienne to do tomorrow morning?

Handy words
sorti tout à l'heure = just went out
donner un message = pass on a message
parler à = speak to
rappeler = to call back

At the Post Office

Q1 Write out these English words a) to f) along with the matching French ones from the box.

a) a stamp d) the Post Office

b) a parcel / package e) a postcard

c) a post box f) a letter

un timbre	**une boîte aux lettres**
une lettre	**la poste**
un paquet	**une carte postale**

Q2 Read this Post Office conversation and answer the questions in English.

René: Bonjour. Je voudrais trois timbres à trente cents et quatre enveloppes.
Assistante: Oui monsieur. Ça fait un euro soixante-dix cents.
René: Voilà. Et je voudrais envoyer ce paquet en Angleterre.
Assistante: Ça vous coûte troi euros cinquante.
René: Où est la boîte aux lettres, s'il vous plaît?
Assistante: Il y en a une ici dans le bureau — la voilà.

a) How many stamps does René want to buy?
b) How much do the stamps and 4 envelopes cost altogether?
c) What does René want to send to England?
d) Is there a letter box in the Post Office?

Q3 Write out what you'd say to ask for each set of stamps in French.

In French you can say either
'un timbre à deux euros' or
'un timbre de deux euros'.

eg *Je voudrais deux timbres à un euro et un timbre à cinquante cents.*

I would like two one euro stamps and one stamp at fifty cents.

a)

One one euro stamp and one thirty cent stamp.

b)

Three one euro stamps and one at fifty cents.

c)

d)

Formal Letters

Q1 Read this letter and answer the questions in English.

> 5 Cherry Lane
> York
> England
>
> Hôtel République
Paris
>
> York, le 3 mai 2000
>
> Madame / Monsieur,
>
> Je voudrais réserver une chambre double chez vous pour quinze jours pendant le mois d'août.
>
> Nous voudrions arriver le 3 août et partir le 17 août.
>
> Je vous prie de bien vouloir me faire savoir combien coûtera la demi-pension.
>
> J'aimerais aussi savoir s'il y a une piscine dans l'hôtel et où nous pourrions garer notre voiture.
>
> Je vous remercie d'avance.
>
> Je vous prie d'agréer l'expression de mes sentiments distingués.
>
> *Jennifer Parker*

*garer la voiture = **park the car**

a) What kind of room does Jennifer want?

b) How long does Jennifer want to go on holiday for?

c) In which month does she want to go?

d) What date does she plan to arrive on?

e) Does she want breakfast included?

f) What two things does Jennifer want to know about the hotel apart from the cost of the room?

Q2 Write out these handy French letter-writing phrases a) to f), along with the matching English one from the oval.

a) Je vous prie d'agréer l'expression de mes sentiments distingués.

b) Je vous remercie d'avance.

c) Je vous serais très reconnaissant(e).

d) Madame / Monsieur,

e) Derby, le 25 février 2001

f) Je vous prie de bien vouloir me renseigner...

> Dear Sir / Madam,
> Many thanks in advance.
> Please give me some information...
> I would be very grateful.
> Derby, 25th February 2001
> Yours sincerely,

Present Tense

Q1 Give the 'je' part of each one of these verbs. They all end in **-er**.

eg donner ➡️ *je donne*

a) manger   d) nager

b) donner   e) jouer

c) montrer   f) commencer

Q2 Write out all the endings for these **-er** verbs using 'donner' to help you.

donner	a) **laisser**	b) **cacher**
je donne	je laiss**e**	je cach**e**
tu donnes	tu laiss...	tu cach...
il/elle donne	il/elle laiss...	il/elle cach...
nous donnons	nous laiss...	nous cach...
vous donnez	vous laiss...	vous cach...
ils/elles donnent	ils/elles laiss...	ils/elles cach...

Q3 Write down the right part of the verb, for a) to h) below.

You can get help for this one from question 2.

eg nager — elle .... ➡️ *elle nage*

a) **nager** — elle ....

b) **emprunter** — nous ....

c) **jouer** — ils ....

d) **donner** — nous ....

e) **manger** — il ....

f) **aimer** — vous ....

g) **montrer** — tu ....

h) **commencer** — je ....

Q4 Write out 'je' with the proper ending for each of these verbs — they all end in **-ir**.

eg finir ➡️ *je fin<u>is</u>*

a) finir   d) vieillir

b) choisir   e) nourrir

c) punir   f) jaunir

Present Tense

Q1   Write out all the parts of **choisir** and **punir**. They go just like **finir**.

<u>finir</u>	a) **choisir**	b) **punir**
je finis	je choisis	je punis
tu finis	tu ...	tu ...
il/elle finit	il/elle ...	il/elle ...
nous finissons	nous ...	nous ...
vous finissez	vous ...	vous ...
ils/elles finissent	ils/elles ...	ils/elles ...

Q2   Write down the right part of the verb for a) to f) below.

You can work out all the answers for this from question 1.

eg finir — vous .... ⟹ *vous finissez*

a) **finir**   — vous ....
b) **choisir**   — nous ....
c) **punir**   — ils ....

d) **nourrir**   — je ....
e) **choisir**   — tu ....
f) **rougir**   — elle ....

Q3   Write out all the parts of **vendre** and **entendre** — use **perdre** to help you.

<u>perdre</u>	a) **vendre**	b) **entendre**
je perds	je vends	j'entends
tu perds	tu ...	tu ...
il/elle perd	il/elle ...	il/elle ...
nous perdons	nous ...	nous ...
vous perdez	vous ...	vous ...
ils/elles perdent	ils/elles ...	ils/elles ...

These ones are called '-re verbs'.

Q4   Write down the right part of the verb for a) to f) below.

eg nous + rendre ⟹ *nous rendons*

a) **rendre**   — nous ....
b) **battre**   — je ....
c) **vendre**   — on ....

d) **attendre**   — vous ....
e) **descendre**   — ils ....
f) **mordre**   — il ....

Irregular Verbs

Q1   Use the right bit of the verb from the box to fill the gaps a) to g).

eg to be = être — I am = je .... ➡️ *suis*

a) to be = **être**   — I am = je ....

b) to have = **avoir**   — you (pl.) have = vous ....

c) to do = **faire**   — you (sing.) are doing = tu ....

d) to be able = **pouvoir** — they can = elles ....

e) to go = **aller**   — we go = nous ....

f) to have to = **devoir** — you (pl.) have to = vous ....

g) to want = **vouloir**   — he wants = il ....

allons	devez	avez
veut	fais	suis
	peuvent	

Look at the words in the box carefully — just match them up with the right words in bold.

Q2   Choose the right verb to finish off each sentence.

eg Les boulangers .... du pain. ➡️ *font*

a) Les boulangers .... du pain. **faites / font**

b) Vous .... plus loin que moi. **allons / allez**

c) Je .... acheter un parapluie. **veux / voulons**

d) Mon frère et moi, nous .... pilotes. **suis / sommes**

e) Est-ce qu'on .... rouler à droite? **dois / doit**

f) Tu ne .... pas dormir dans le salle de bain. **peux / peut**

Q3   Match the verb in **bold** from each sentence with the right word from the oval.

*eg Ils **doivent** attendre le train prochain.* ➡️ *devoir*

avoir
aller
devoir
être
pouvoir
vouloir

a) Ils **doivent** attendre le train prochain.

b) Je **vais** à la piscine tous les mercredis et vendredis.

c) Je ne **peux** pas vous aider.

d) Marc **veut** rendre visite à sa grand-mère.

e) Mon oncle **a** douze chats.

f) Vous **êtes** plus laids que lourds.

Je ne peux pas vous aider.

In the Past — Perfect Tense

Q1   These **-er** verbs are all in the present tense. Write them out so they're in the past.

eg il mange ⟹ il a mangé

he eats   he ate

Use the right bits of 'avoir' — j'ai, tu as, il/elle a, nous avons, vous avez, ils/elles ont.

a) il mange
b) tu danses
c) elles bavardent
d) j'achète
e) nous cachons
f) ils trouvent
g) elle joue
h) vous cherchez

Q2   Do the same thing with these **-ir** verbs. Write them out so they're in the past tense.

eg tu finis ⟹ tu as fini

you finish   you finished

a) tu finis
b) nous dormons
c) je choisis
d) elles punissent
e) je dors
f) vous finissez
g) il nourrit
h) tu choisis

Q3   Same again — put these **-re** verbs into the perfect tense.

Thanks - you can have it back now.

eg vous rendez ⟹ vous avez rendu

you (pl.) give back   you gave back

a) vous rendez
b) elle vend
c) ils attendent
d) nous perdons
e) je mords
f) elles correspondent
g) tu rends
h) il attend

Q4   Swap the English bit in each sentence with the right bit from the box, then write out the whole French sentence (and I mean the **whole** sentence).

eg **He sold** + la voiture. ⟹ Il a vendu la voiture.

a) **He sold**   +   la voiture.
b) **He's finished**   +   ses devoirs.
c) **I gave**   +   le stylo à Jean.
d) **We looked for**   +   le lion.
e) **She's bought**   +   une CD.
f) **They danced**   +   hier soir.
g) **She hid**   +   la fourchette sous la table.
h) **You** (pl.) **chose** + un bon film.

> nous avons cherché
> elle a acheté
> ils ont dansé
> vous avez choisi
> il a fini
> elle a caché
> il a vendu
> j'ai donné

Perfect tense with 'avoir' and 'être'

Q1 Translate these sentences into French. All you need to do is fill in the missing bits with the right form of the verb **avoir** from the box.

 eg I played golf. ➡ *J'ai joué au golf.*

a) I ate an apple.   *J'..... mangé une pomme.*

b) Elise left her coat on the chair.   *Elise .... laissé son manteau sur la chaise.*

c) We listened to Bob.   *Nous ...... écouté Bob.*

d) You played the piano.   *Tu ..... joué du piano.*

e) You bought some pens.   *Vous ..... acheté des stylos.*

ai	avons
as	avez
a	ont

Q2 Some annoying verbs take **être** instead of **avoir**.

*They **all** go like this.*

Je suis allé(e)   Nous sommes allé(e)s
Tu es allé(e)   Vous êtes allé(e)s
Il est allé   Ils sont allés
Elle est allée.   Elles sont allées.

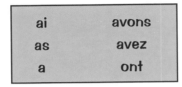

There's an extra e when you're talking about someone female.

There's an extra s when there's more than one person.

Write out these verbs in the past tense. Use **aller** to help you.

a) arriver

b) rester

Q3 Translate these sentences into French. Most of it's already done — all you need to do is write them out and fill in the missing bits with the right verbs from the box.

 eg Suzanne went upstairs. ➡ *Suzanne est montée.*

Watch out for extra e and s.

a) I danced with Sylvie.   *J' .... avec Sylvie.*

b) Greg sold his car to Louise.   *Greg .... sa voiture à Louise.*

c) We got off the train.   *Nous .... du train.*

d) You got back home at 11pm.   *Tu .... à la maison à vingt-trois heures.*

e) Marie and Christine went to Italy.   *Marie et Christine .... en Italie.*

a vendu	ai dansé	sommes descendues
	es rentré	sont allées est montée

Irregular Perfect Tense

Q1 Which of the words in the box would you use if you were writing these verbs in the past tense?

a) prendre
b) mettre
c) boire
d) écrire
e) dire
f) voir
g) lire
h) venir

écrit
bu
lu
vu
venu
pris
mis
dit

Perfect!

Q2 Translate these sentences into French. All you need to do is pick the right word from the brackets, and write the whole sentence out in French. Easy really.

a) I drank a glass of water.   *J'(ai buvu / ai bu) un verre d'eau*
b) Bill wrote a letter.   *Bill (a écrivé / a écrit) une lettre.*
c) We ran very fast to the station.   *Nous (avons couru / avons couri) très vite à la gare.*
d) He put on his hat.   *Il (a mis / a metté) son chapeau.*
e) You've read that book.   *Vous (avez lisé / avez lu) ce livre.*
f) I said goodbye to Lauren.   *J'(ai dit / ai disé) au revoir à Lauren.*

Q3 The past tense verbs are missing from these French sentences. Choose the right verbs from the box to fill the gaps, and write out all the sentences. Use the English translations to help you work them out.

a) Brian et Steve .... rester au pub.   *Brian and Steve wanted to stay at the pub.*
b) Gaelle .... voir les chiens.   *Gaelle has come to see the dogs.*
c) J' .... ta lettre.   *I received your letter.*
d) Nous .... qu'il faisait froid.   *We said that it was cold.*
e) Mary .... un petit agneau.   *Mary had a little lamb.*
f) Sally .... du fromage sur ses frites.   *Sally put some cheese on her chips.*

est venue	a eu	a mis	
ai reçu		avons dit	ont voulu

Reflexive Verbs

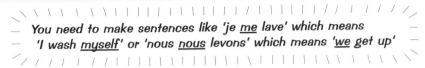

Q1 Pick the right word from the two choices in **bold**. Write out each sentence in full.

*You need to make sentences like 'je __me__ lave' which means
'I wash __myself__' or 'nous __nous__ levons' which means '__we__ get up'*

a) Je **me/moi** lève à huit heures.

b) Caroline **se/es** sent mal.

c) Nous **se/nous** amusons.

d) Tu **toi/te** brosses les dents.

e) Vous **ve/vous** intéressez aux bières belges.

f) Ils **se/ont** couchent à minuit.

g) Ma tante **s'/s'est** appelle Poonam.

Q2 Write out all the forms of **se coucher**. It's dead easy, because it follows the same pattern as **se trouver**.

All reflexive verbs go like this.

je me trouve	nous nous trouvons
tu te trouves	vous vous trouvez
il se trouve	ils se trouvent
elle se trouve	elles se trouvent
on se trouve	

Q3 Translate these sentences into French. Part of it's already done, which is nice. You need to choose the right verbs from the box to fill in each of the gaps.

te laves	se lève	vous intéressez
me sens		
	s'appelle	nous excusons
s'écrit	se trouve	s'amusent

a) Marie gets up at half past seven. *Marie .... à sept heures et demie.*

b) I feel ill. *Je .... mal.*

c) This is my friend. He's called Pascal. *Voici mon ami. Il .... Pascal.*

d) We're sorry for arriving so late. *Nous .... d'arriver si tard.*

e) Are you interested in table tennis? *Vous .... au tennis de table?*

f) This word is difficult — how is it spelt? *Ce mot est difficile — comment ça .... ?*

g) The children are having fun. *Les enfants· ....*

h) Do you wash before you go to school? *Tu .... avant d'aller au collège?*

i) Where is Saint Michel church? *Où .... l'église Saint Michel?*

Reflexive Past Tense

Q1 Translate these sentences into English. The English translations are all in the box underneath, so it's really just a case of matching them up and writing them out.

eg *Je me suis levé.* *I got up.*

a) Je me suis intéressé aux films étrangers.

b) Nous nous sommes beaucoup amusés.

c) Tu t'es lavé.

d) Elle s'est brossée les dents.

e) Ils se sont excusés.

f) Vous vous êtes levés.

g) Elle s'est réveillée.

h) Il s'est lavé.

i) Il s'est senti mal.

j) Nous nous sommes couchés.

He felt ill.	**We went to bed.**
I was interested in foreign films	**You got up.**
You washed yourself.	**She brushed her teeth.**
They were sorry	**We had a lot of fun.**
He washed himself.	**She woke up**

Q2 Fill in the right endings for these verbs. Remember that the endings need an extra **e** for females and an extra **s** when it's more than one person.

a) Il s'est couché...

b) Elles se sont couché...

c) Nous (female) nous sommes couché...

d) Elle s'est couché...

e) Ils se sont couché...

f) Vous (male, singular) vous êtes couché...

g) Vous (female, plural) vous êtes couché...

h) Je (female) me suis couché...

i) Je (male) me suis couché...

Couché!

You won't need to add an e or an s to every single one.

Future using Aller

Q1   You can talk about the future in French using the verb **aller** (to go), kind of like we do in English. You can say you're 'going to' do something. Match the French sentences with their English translations.

eg   1) Je vais jouer au tennis. ⟹ **D) I'm going to play tennis.**

1) Je vais jouer au tennis.

2) Dimanche, nous allons aller au cinéma.

3) La semaine prochaine, elle va danser.

4) Ce soir, je vais regarder la télévision.

5) Après le film, mes amis vont manger de la pizza.

6) Vous allez faire le shopping ce matin.

7) Il va faire la vaisselle.

A) You're going to do the shopping this morning.

B) She's going dancing next week.

C) He's going to do the washing up.

D) I'm going to play tennis.

E) After the film my friends are going to eat pizza.

F) On Sunday we're going to the cinema.

G) I'm going to watch TV this evening.

Q2   Choose the right verb from the box to fill in the gap in each French sentence, and write out the whole sentence. Use the English translations to help you.

eg Je vais ...... l'aspirateur. ⟹ *Je vais __passer__ l'aspirateur.*
      I'm going to vacuum.

| faire | aller | manger |
| passer | ranger | aller |

a) Je vais .... l'aspirateur.   *I'm going to vacuum.*

b) Il va .... sa chambre.   *He's going to tidy his room.*

c) Nous allons .... beaucoup de chocolat.   *We're going to eat a lot of chocolate.*

d) Vous allez .... au parc avec votre chien.   *You're going to go to the park with your dog.*

e) Demain, tu vas .... du ski.   *You are going to go skiing tomorrow.*

f) Elles vont .... au théâtre.   *They are going to go to the theatre.*

Q3   More future tense sentences, but this time I've left out the bits of **aller**. Choose the right bit of **aller** from the frog and write out the whole French sentence.

a) Cette nuit, je .... écouter mon nouveau CD.   *Tonight I'm going to listen to my new CD.*

b) Mardi, nous .... visiter le musée.   *On Tuesday we are going to visit the museum.*

c) En juin, vous .... acheter un chien.   *In June you're going to buy a dog.*

d) Vendredi, il .... voir le médecin.   *On Thursday he's going to see the doctor.*

e) Elles .... chanter.   *They are going to sing.*

f) Tu .... aller à l'école.   *You are going to go to school.*

va vais
allez
vas   vont
allons

Future Tense

The boxes show you the endings verbs get to make them future tense. They should help you with this page.

Future tense endings:	
je ...ai	nous ...ons
tu ...as	vous ...ez
il/elle ...a	ils/elles ...ont

eg jouer	
je jouerai	*nous jouerons*
tu joueras	*vous jouerez*
il/elle jouera	*ils/elles joueront*

Q1 Write out these French sentences and underline the future tense verb.

eg *Je pourrai le faire.* ⟹ *Je <u>pourrai</u> le faire.*

a) Je pourrai le faire.　　　　　　　　　　I'll be able to do that.

b) Nous devrons faire nos devoirs.　　　We'll have to do our homework.

c) Je ferai mes devoirs.　　　　　　　　　I'll do my homework.

d) Il voudra venir avec nous.　　　　　　He'll want to come with us.

e) Je viendrai avec vous.　　　　　　　　I'll come with you.

f) J'aurai beaucoup de temps.　　　　　　I'll have lots of time.

Q2 I've left the French verbs out of these sentences about the future. There are two options for each gap. Choose the right verb and write out the full French sentences.

a) Demain, nous *(will buy)* une voiture.　　　　　　　　　　　**achèterons / achetons**

b) On *(will listen to)* un concert.　　　　　　　　　　　　　　**écouteras / écoutera**

c) Je te *(will give)* toutes les informations.　　　　　　　　**donnai / donnerai**

d) Elles *(will sleep)* pendant dix heures.　　　　　　　　　　**dormiras / dormiront**

e) Tu *(will forget)* les lettres.　　　　　　　　　　　　　　　**oublieras / oublas**

f) Vous *(will ask)* s'il est permis d'apporter les chiens.　　**demandez / demanderez**

g) Je *(will finish)* par raconter une histoire amusante.　　　**fini / finirai**

h) Ils *(will write)* un article pour le magazine.　　　　　　　**écri / écriront**

i) Elle *(will eat)* tous les gâteaux.　　　　　　　　　　　　　**manga / mangera**

Q3 This is a bit tricky now. Write out these these sentences in English. Use a dictionary if you can't remember a word.

eg *J'enverrai une lettre.* ⟹ *I'm going to send a letter.*

a) J'enverrai une lettre.

b) Il ne saura pas.

c) Il faudra aller à la poste.

d) Elle tiendra une rose dans la main.

Imperfect Tense

Q1   Here are some sentences about the past in the imperfect tense. I've left **il y avait** out of them all. Follow the example and write out all the sentences in full.

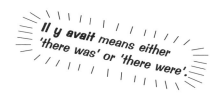

Il y avait means either 'there was' or 'there were'.

eg *............. un grand cochon devant la maison.* ⟶ *Il y avait un grand cochon devant la maison.*

There was a big pig in front of the house.

a) .... beaucoup à faire à Londres.   *There was a lot to do in London.*
b) .... cinq femmes et quatre hommes.   *There were five women and four men.*
c) .... un singe dans l'arbre.   *There was a monkey in the tree.*
d) Hier .... du vent.   *Yesterday it was windy.*
e) Au parc, ... dix canards.   *In the park there were ten ducks.*

Q2   These past tense sentences have got **c'était** missing.
Follow the example and write out all the sentences in full.

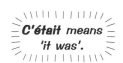

C'était means 'it was'.

eg *............. un grand cochon rose.* ⟹ *C'était un grand cochon rose.*

It was a big pink pig.

a) .... trop cher.   **It was too expensive.**

b) .... très beau.   **It was very beautiful.**

c) .... assez grand et effrayant.   **It was very big and scary.**

d) .... le premier mars dix-neuf quatre-vingt-cinq.   **It was the first of March 1985.**

Q3   Some of these sentences are written in the present tense and others in the imperfect tense. Write out each one, underline the verb then write which tense it is.

eg *Je regardais la télévision.* ⟹ *Je <u>regardais</u> la télévision. Imperfect tense.*
I watched the television.

a) Je regardais la télévision.
b) Il fait un grand bruit.
c) Nous attendions le facteur.

d) Elle danse dans la salle à manger.
e) Il tenait un papier dans la main.
f) Tu nettoyais la chambre.
g) Je buvais un café.
h) Vous jouez du badminton.
i) Je jouais du piano.

Negatives

Q1 Turn these sentences from positive to negative. Just follow the example.

eg *J'aime les chiens* *Je n'aime pas les chiens.*
I like dogs.   I don't like dogs.

a) Je mange la banane. I eat the banana.
b) Nous lavons nos vêtements. We wash our clothes.
c) C'est loin d'ici. It's a long way from here.
d) Il lit un livre. He's reading a book.
e) C'est la même chose. It's the same.
f) Sandrine est ma soeur. Sandrine is my sister.
g) Je prépare le déjeuner. I am preparing lunch.
h) J'ai des pommes. I have some apples.

Sometimes you will need to do more than put in ne & pas — 'des' becomes 'de' in a negative sentence and you say 'pas de' rather than 'pas un'.

Q2 Write down the French sentences a) - h) matched up with their English meaning. There are some useful little negative phrases in the box to help you.

ne .... jamais	**never**	ne .... personne	**nobody**
ne .... rien	**nothing**	ne .... ni .... ni	**neither nor**
ne .... plus	**not any more**	ne .... aucun(e)	**not any, not one**

a) Nous n'avons plus de pommes. You're not making any effort.
b) Il n'est jamais là. There is nothing to do in Jamaisville.
c) Je ne joue ni au football ni au tennis. I've never seen that man.
d) Tu ne fais aucun effort. He's never there.
e) Il n'y a rien à faire à Jamaisville. I play neither football nor tennis.
f) Personne n'aime ta jupe orange. We don't have any apples left.
g) Je n'ai jamais vu cet homme. Nobody likes your orange skirt.

Q3 Write out the English meanings of these sentences. This is harder than before, but all the sentences are pretty easy really.

a) Je ne vais plus à La Rochelle.
b) Je ne vais jamais à La Rochelle.
c) Je ne vais ni à La Rochelle ni à Nice.
d) Il n'y a personne ici.

Crikey — what <u>do</u> you look like in that skirt?!

Savoir, Connaître, Pouvoir

Q1 Put these sentences into French by filling in the gaps with the right bit of the verb **savoir**, which is written out in a box for you. Write the sentences out in full.

eg I <u>know</u> where you are. Je <u>sais</u> où vous êtes.

a) She knows where the fish shop is.
   Elle ..... où se trouve la poissonnerie.

b) I don't know.
   Je ne ..... pas.

c) We know a lot about ancient civilizations.
   Nous ..... beaucoup de choses sur les civilisations anciennes.

d) Do you know when the next train leaves?
   .....-vous à quelle heure part le premier train?

e) Do you know who won the competition?
   Tu ..... qui a gagné la compétition?

Savoir means 'to know a fact'

je sais	nous savons
tu sais	vous savez
il/elle sait	ils/elles savent

Q2 Stick the right bit of **pouvoir** into each of these sentences. Use the English translation of each sentence to help you.

eg Je peux aller chez toi. I can go to your house.

a) Est-ce que tu ..... m'aider?
   Can you help me?

b) Je ne ..... pas venir ce soir.
   I can't come tonight.

c) Ils ..... jouer au tennis cet après-midi.
   They can play tennis this afternoon.

d) Nous ..... dîner avant dix-neuf heures.
   We can eat dinner before 7pm.

e) Vous ..... porter mes valises.
   You can carry my suitcases.

Pouvoir means 'to be able to'.

je peux	nous pouvons
tu peux	vous pouvez
il peut	ils peuvent

Q3 Put these sentences into French. Wherever there's a gap, pop in the right bit of the verb **connaître** from the box.

eg He <u>knows</u> Jim. Il <u>connaît</u> Jim.

a) Do you know my sister?
   Tu ..... ma soeur?

b) He doesn't know that book.
   Il ne ..... pas ce livre.

c) We know Orléans very well.
   Nous ..... très bien Orléans.

d) Do you know this town?
   Vous ..... cette ville?

e) I know Megan. *Je ..... Megan.*

Connaître means 'to know a person or a place'.

je connais	nous connaissons
tu connais	vous connaissez
il connaît	ils connaissent

Imperative/ Present Participle

Q1   Translate these sentences into French, putting in the right verbs from the box.

eg _Sell the guitar!_   ⟹   _Vendez la guitare!_

eg _Let's take a brolly!_   ⟹   _Prenons un parapluie!_

a) Finish your homework!   ..... _tes devoirs!_

b) Let's go to the ice rink!   ..... _à la patinoire!_

c) Francine and Agnès, come with us!   _Francine et Agnès, ... avec nous!_

d) Eat your vegetables!   ..... _tes légumes!_

e) Let's make lots of noise!   ..... _beaucoup de bruit!_

f) Take the first road on the left.   ..... _la première rue à gauche._

g) Try once more! (to a friend)   ..... _encore une fois!_

All you've got to do is pick the right verb. It's not that hard.

Prenez	Faisons	Essaie
Finis		
Allons	Venez	Mange

Q2   Put these sentences into French, using the right **-ant** verb from the box.

eg _He sings while reading the paper_   ⟹   _Il chante en lisant le journal._

a) I played the piano while talking. _J'ai joué du piano en ....._

b) He gives her the baton while running. _Il lui donne le bâton en ....._

c) She came in screaming. _Elle est entrée en ....._

d) She was looking at me while dancing. _Elle me régardait en ....._

e) I lost my hat while returning home. _J'ai perdu mon chapeau en ..... à la maison._

dansant	parlant	courant	rentrant	criant

Q3   Write out all the verbs on list A. Next to each one, write the -ant verb from list B that goes with it.

**All** of the -ant verbs start off the same as the **nous** bit of the present tense.

List A

a) donner
b) faire
c) finir
d) aller
e) boire
f) dire

List B

finissant
faisant
allant
buvant
disant
donnant

Articles and Gender

Q1 Write out all these words, and put 'un' or 'une' in front of each one, depending on whether it's masculine or feminine.

If you don't know, use a dictionary. It's not cheating, you know.

a) chat
b) chien
c) maison
d) salle
e) table
f) chaise
g) cheval

h) livre
i) stylo
j) image
k) banane
l) gâteau
m) tasse
n) thé

o) café
p) ville
q) village
r) ordinateur
s) papier
t) verre
u) bouteille

v) journal
w) nation
x) pays
y) orange
z) haricot

Q2 Put **le**, **la** or **l'** in front of each of these nouns depending on whether it's masculine, feminine or starts with a vowel. For the **l'** ones, add (m) or (f) after the noun to show whether it's masculine or feminine.

a) cassette
b) arbre
c) bateau
d) oignon
e) hôtel
f) haricot

g) bonheur
h) rue
i) hockey
j) oreille
k) tête
l) main

m) pied
n) auberge
o) histoire
p) hors-d'oeuvre
q) chocolat
r) eau

Some nouns beginning with 'h' have l' in front of them, but some have le or la.

Q3 List A is a list of women's job titles. Write out all the jobs from list A. Next to each one, write the men's version of the job title from list B.

eg *la factrice* *le facteur*

the postwoman → *the postman*

List A

a) La boulangère
b) La coiffeuse
c) La comptable
d) La dentiste
e) La factrice
f) L'institutrice
g) L'infirmière
h) La pharmacienne
i) La secrétaire
j) La vendeuse

List B

L'infirmier
Le facteur
Le boulanger
Le comptable
Le secrétaire
Le dentiste
Le pharmacien
Le vendeur
L'instituteur
Le coiffeur

Hmmm, egg tester, £15 per hour...

__Plurals__

Q1 Plural means more than one. Make each of these words plural.
Basically, you're just changing 'the thing' to 'the things', but in French. Obviously.

eg *le chien* ⟹ *les chiens*

the dog the dogs

You looking at me?

Le and la both turn into les when there's more than one .

- a) l'adresse
- b) la banane
- c) le cinéma
- d) le dépliant
- e) la famille

- f) le jardin
- g) le légume
- h) la plage
- i) le robinet
- j) le supermarché

Q2 Some words that end in u or l have weird plurals — the endings change completely.
Write out the proper plural for each of these words.

eg *le journal* ⟹ *les journaux*

the newspaper the newspapers

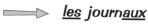

*All you have to do is pick the right ending from the brackets,
and write the whole word out. Don't forget the 'les'.*

- a) le château (aux/aus)
- b) le journal (als/aux)
- c) le jeu (oux/eux)
- d) le chapeau (aux/aus)
- e) le feu (eus/eux)
- f) le neveu (aux/eux)
- g) le cheval (als/aux)
- h) le genou (oux/aux)

- i) le chou (ous/oux)
- j) le canal (aux/als)
- k) le cheveu (eaux/aux)
- l) le travail (aix/aux)
- m) l'eau (aux/aus)
- n) le bureau (oux/aux)
- o) le bijou (oux/aux)
- p) le morceau (eux/eaux)

Q3 Write out all the words a) to g). Next to each one, write the matching plural from the box.

- a) un jeu
- b) un cheval
- c) un travail
- d) un feu
- e) un oeil
- f) un bureau
- g) une voix

des bureaux

des feux

des voix

des travaux

des jeux

des chevaux des yeux

À and de

Q1 Pick the right word to finish each sentence, and write the whole thing out in French.

> eg Je vais .... collège en voiture. ⟹ Je vais <u>au</u> collège en voiture.

a) Je vais .... collège en voiture. **au aux**

b) Je vais .... Paris cette année. **à la à**

c) On peut encaisser des chèques .... banque. **aux à la**

d) Ce livre est .... Michel. **à à la**

e) Je déjeune .... midi. **à à la**

f) Je l'ai vu .... télévision. **au à la**

g) Cet après-midi, on va .... jardin zoologique. **au aux**

> à + la = à la
> à + le = au
> à + les = aux

> Plain 'à' goes in front of words which don't get a 'le' or 'la', like cities and people.

Q2 Now fill the gaps in these sentences with **à**, **à la**, **au** or **aux**.

a) Nous allons donner des bonbons .... enfants.

b) Je nage tous les jours .... piscine.

c) Il s'intéresse .... tennis de table.

d) Je fais toutes mes courses .... supermarché.

e) Vous allez .... aéroport pour rencontrer votre tante.

f) Il veut aller .... Londres.

g) Ce chien, il est .... Jeanne.

Q3 Choose the right words to finish off sentences a) to h).

> eg *Voulez-vous de/du sucre?* ⟹ *Voulez-vous <u>du</u> sucre?*

a) J'ai acheté **du/des** pommes de terre au marché.

b) Avez vous **du/de la** chocolat?

c) C'est la voiture **du/de** Marie.

d) Je n'ai pas **de/de la** pain.

e) Tu as **de la/des** oranges.

f) Je suis très content **de la/de** voir ce film.

g) Je n'ai pas **de/des** bananes.

h) Il écrit **de/des** bons livres.

More Prepositions

Q1 These sentences have all got **en** in. Translate them into English.
Look in the box if you need help with vocab.

a) Je vais en France.

b) J'habite en Angleterre.

c) Je vais en Espagne.

> *j'y vais* — I'm going there
> *cuir rouge* — red leather

d) Je suis en vacances.

e) Marie-Thérèse va au collège en voiture.

f) Aujourd'hui, je vais en ville.

g) J'y vais en bus.

h) Mon sac est en cuir rouge.

i) Le sac de Martine est en plastique.

Q2 Match the French words a), b) and c) up with the right English meaning from the box.

a) pour

b) depuis

c) à partir de

> **since / for**
> **from**
> **for**

Q3 These sentences have got **pour**, **depuis**, or **à partir de** in them.
Translate them into English. If you don't know a word it might be in the box.

a) Le train pour Calais a dix minutes de retard.

b) C'est un cadeau pour toi.

c) Je suis venu ici pour voir mon frère.

d) J'apprends le français depuis quatre ans.

e) Il est ici depuis dix heures.

> *en retard* — late
> *un cadeau* — a present
> *la bibliothèque* — the library

f) La bibliothèque sera fermée à partir du 6 juillet.

g) C'est trop tard pour aller au cinéma.

h) Je lis ce livre depuis hier.

More Prepositions

Q1 Match the French words up with the right English ones from the box.
The first three are already done.

a) sous — *under*

b) sur — *on*

c) dans — *in*

d) derrière —

e) devant —

f) contre —

g) entre —

> behind
> on
> in front of
> in
> between
> under
> against

Q2 Translate sentences a) to h) into English.
They've all got one of the words from Q1 in, so use it to help you.

a) Le chien est sous le lit.

b) Hélène est dans la salle à manger.

c) Je joue du tennis contre Bernard.

d) Le marché se trouve devant la mairie.

e) J'ai mis le chou-fleur sur la table.

f) Marguerite est derrière la porte.

g) Xavier est assis entre Christophe et Émilie.

h) Annelise écrit un article sur Napoléon.

> *la salle à manger* — the dining room *le chou-fleur* — the cauliflower
> *la mairie* — town hall *assis* — sitting

Q3 The box tells you the meanings of some more French phrases about where things are.
Use it to turn these sentences into English ones.

a) L'église se trouve **en face de** la piscine.

b) Les toilettes se trouvent **au bout du** couloir.

c) Mon collège se trouve **à côté d'**un parc.

d) Le portrait est **au-dessus de** l'étagère.

e) Mon professeur est **au fond de** la salle de classe.

f) Mon pupitre est **au-dessous de** la fenêtre.

g) La poste est **à côté des** feux.

h) La boucherie est **en face de** la pâtisserie.

> *au bout de* — at the end of
> *au fond de* — at the back of
> *à côté de* — beside
> *en face de* — opposite
> *au-dessous de* — below
> *au-dessus de* — above

If you have trouble telling these apart remember 'sous' means 'under'.

<u>Conjunctions</u>

Q1   Conjunctions are words like 'and' and 'but' that join bits of sentences together.
      Match these French conjunctions up with the right English words from the cloud.

a) et   e) car   i) donc

b) ou   f) si   j) pendant

c) mais   g) avec   k) pendant que

d) presque   h) comme   l) alors

while   during   because
    if   nearly   like
and   so   with
therefore   or
but

Q2   Choose the right word to finish off each sentence,
      and write the whole thing out in French.

a) J'ai mangé deux bananes .... trois melons. **pendant   et**

b) Je veux me promener .... il pleut. **comme   mais**

c) Je voudrais un café .... du sucre. **avec   car**

d) Sylvie est .... sa soeur. **donc   comme**

e) .... le match, nous sommes restés à la maison. **et   pendant**

f) Tu peux venir ce soir, ... tu veux. **si   presque**

Q3   Choose a word out of the box to fill the gaps in a) to g).
      Don't just write the words down — write the whole sentence.

You only need to use each word once — should make life easier.

a) Je n'aime pas le hockey, ... c'est trop fatigant.

b) Robert et Chantelle vont .... nous.

c) Je reste ici .... tu achètes des légumes.

d) Elle veut voir un film d'amour, ... je préfère les films comiques.

e) .... nous sortons je porte mon pull rouge.

f) J'aime la musique rock, ... toi.

g) Il était pâtissier .... la guerre.

mais	parce que	pendant
si	avec	
pendant que		comme

<u>Adjectives</u>

Q1   Write out these phrases in French using the word **grand** with the right endings on it.

   eg *The big bag.* ⟹ *Le grand sac.*

   Grand comes <u>before</u> the word it's describing.

   a) The big dog.

   b) The big house.

   c) The big books.

   d) The big trees.

   e) The big ears.

m. sing.	f. sing.	m. pl.	f. pl.
gran<u>d</u>	grand<u>e</u>	grand<u>s</u>	grand<u>es</u>

Look up any words you don't know.

Q2   Write out these phrases in French using the word **vert** with the right endings.

   eg *The green bag.* ⟹ *Le sac vert.*

   Most French adjectives go <u>after</u> the word they are describing.

   a) The green mountain.   d) The green apples.

   b) The green coat.   e) The green man.

   c) The green eyes.   f) The green lettuce.

Q3   Adjectives which end in **-eux** are a bit different. Write out the sentences a) to n) putting the right endings on the adjective each time. Use this table to work out what the ending should be.

il	elle	ils	elles
heureu<u>x</u>	heureu<u>se</u>	heureu<u>x</u>	heureu<u>ses</u>

*Sérieux, ennuyeux, délicieux, dangereux and merveilleux all take the same endings as **heureux**.*

   eg *Un garçon heur...* ⟹ *Un garçon heureux.*

   a) Un garçon heur...   h) Des films merveill...

   b) Une fille heur...   i) Des choses séri...

   c) Des livres séri...   j) Des hommes danger...

   d) Un repas délici...   k) Une matière ennuy...

   e) Des gâteaux délici...   l) Des profs ennuy...

   f) Des rues danger...   m) Ton frère est ennuy...

   g) Une histoire merveill...   n) Mes soeurs sont ennuy...

Adjectives

Q1 Write out sentences a) to k) in English. There's an irregular adjective in each one. The box on the right shows you the different forms of each adjective used here.

a) Elle est une belle femme.

b) J'ai de nouveaux vêtements.

c) Tes amis sont fous.

d) J'ai une vieille tante.

nouveau	beau	fou	vieux
nouvel	bel	fol	vieil
nouvelle	belle	folle	vieille
nouveaux	beaux	fous	vieux
nouvelles	belles	folles	vieilles

e) Ces idées sont folles.

f) Jean-Jacques est un bel homme.

g) J'ai de nouvelles chaussures.

h) Ce vieil homme est mon grand-père.

i) J'ai acheté un bel éléphant.

j) Les montagnes sont belles!

k) Mes grand-parents sont vieux.

Q2 Write down sentences a) to g) filling in the gap in each sentence with the right word from the box.

eg ..... *mes amis sont ici.* *Tous mes amis sont ici.*

a) ..... mes amis sont ici.

b) Elle a des cheveux .....

c) J'aime les toilettes .....

d) Cette rue est très .....

e) ..... les bananes sont brunes.

f) Je reste ici pendant ..... la journée.

g) Ces pièces de théâtre sont trop .....

longs
longue
longues
toutes
toute
tous
publiques

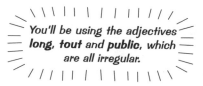
You'll be using the adjectives *long*, *tout* and **public**, which are all irregular.

Q3 Write out these sentences in English.

Look up any words you don't know.

a) Elle est une fille très triste.

b) Ces questions sont difficiles.

c) Ma voiture est rapide, mais ta voiture est lente.

d) J'aime les films intéressants.

e) Ces filles ne sont pas normales.

f) Je n'aime pas les vélos lents.

All these adjectives — like most adjectives — go *after* the noun.

Comparative and Superlative

Q1 Write out sentences a) to d).
Follow the example and fill in the final words each time.

eg Jean est <u>grand</u>, mais Philippe est <u>plus grand</u>.

Jean is tall, but Philippe is taller.

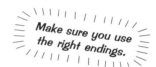

a) Sylvie est <u>gentille</u>, mais Marie est .....

b) M Renard est <u>intéressant</u>, mais Henri est .....

c) Mes souris sont <u>blanches</u>, mais tes souris sont .....

d) Tes livres sont <u>beaux</u>, mais mes livres sont .....

Q2 Write out these sentences. Fill each gap with one of the options given in brackets.

Make sure you use the right endings.

a) Sylvie est gentille, mais Sébastien est ..... (plus gentille / plus gentil)

b) Sandrine est belle, mais tes soeurs sont .... (plus belles / plus belle)

c) Tes histoires sont ennuyeuses, mais ce livre est encore ..... (plus ennuyeuse / plus ennuyeux)

d) Mon poulet est jeune, mais les poulets d'Yvette sont ..... (plus jeune / plus jeunes)

e) Ton pantalon est vert, mais la pelouse est encore ..... (plus vert / plus verte)

Q3 Write out these sentences and fill in the gaps using **le plus**, **la plus** or **les plus**.

eg Hugo est <u>le plus grand</u>.
Hugo is the tallest.

a) Hugo est ..... grand.

b) Jeanne est ..... grande.

c) Hugo et Jeanne sont ..... grands.

d) Je suis étrange, mais il est ..... étrange.

e) Cet arbre est ..... vert.

f) Mary est ..... petite.

g) Ce livre est ..... intéressant.

h) Ces pommes sont ..... rouges.

Q4 Use the words in the box to fill in the gaps in a) - f) and write out a complete French sentence for each.

a) Mon livre est (better than) ton livre.

b) Les livres sont (worse than) les films.

c) Il est (the best).

d) Je suis (the best) actrice.

e) John est (the worst) acteur.

f) Les bananes jaunes sont (the best) bananes.

mieux (que)
pire (que)

le meilleur
la meilleure
les meilleur(e)s
le/la/les pire(s)

Adverbs

Q1 Write out the French sentences a) to e) using the right word from the box to complete each one. Only use each word once.

Ugh. Late again. It just doesn't get dark early enough in summer.

a) Il marche .....
He walks slowly.

b) ....., nous n'avons pas perdu le chien.
Luckily we haven't lost the dog.

c) Ton cadeau m'a fait .... plaisir!
I really like your present.

d) Ce film est ...... étrange.
The film is really strange.

e) ..., je me lève à huit heures.
Normally I get up at eight o'clock.

> lentement
>
> normalement
>
> heureusement
>
> énormément
>
> vraiment

Q2 Write out the sentences a) to f). Choose the right word from the two choices to replace the bit that's still in English.

a) Il marche toujours **slowly** au collège.   **lentement / mal**

b) **Luckily**, elle n'attendait pas depuis longtemps!   **bien / heureusement**

c) Il est **really** sympa!   **très / vraiment**

d) **Honestly**, je ne me souviens pas de ce film.   **vraiment / fièrement**

e) Traverse la route **carefully**.   **vite / prudemment**

f) **Unfortunately**, il est parti la semaine dernière.   **malheureusement / dangereusement**

Q3 Choose the right word from the oval to complete each sentence and write the whole thing out.

Watch out, there are more words here than you need.

a) Il n'est (simply) jamais arrivé.

b) Fais tes devoirs (correctly)!

c) Parle plus (softly), le bébé dort!

d) J'ai trouvé le chemin très (easily).

e) Est-ce que tu peux aller chercher du pain, (quickly) s'il te plaît?

f) Ma soeur a (totally) oublié de te téléphoner!

> facilement   fièrement
> correctement   rapidement
> simplement   bien   totalement
> malheureusement   doucement
> lentement

More Adverbs

Q1   Translate these sentences into English. The harder
bits of vocab are in a box to make things easier.

eg Tu as <u>mal</u> entendu. ➡ *You didn't hear properly.*

a) Il ne se sent pas bien.

b) Je n'ai pas bien compris.

c) Ce que tu as fait est mal.

d) La route était mal indiquée.

e) Ta chambre est mal rangée.

f) Il a bien mangé aujourd'hui.

> **Il se sent — he feels**
> **J'ai compris — I have understood**
> **Ce que — the thing that**
> **tu as fait — you did**
>
> **La route — the road**
> **indiquée — shown**
> **rangée — arranged/tidied**
> **aujourd'hui — today**

Q2   Translate these sentences into English. Use the vocab from the box to help.

eg Il est <u>presque</u> midi. ➡ *It's nearly midday.*

a) J'ai trop mangé ce soir.

b) Tu as presque fini.

c) J'ai assez travaillé pour aujourd'hui.

d) Il fait très beau.

e) Je n'ai pas assez d'argent.

f) Vous avez bu trop de bière.

g) Ta robe est très belle.

h) Ton frère est très sympa.

> **J'ai travaillé — I've worked**
> **presque — nearly**
>
> **d'argent — money**
> **sympa — nice**

Q3   Pick the right word to finish off each French sentence. There's an English translation
to help you, so all you have to do is pick the word that means the right thing.

a) Il a fini son travail plus **rapidement/lentement** que son frère.
    He finished his work more quickly than his brother.

b) Tu te sens **mieux/assez**, Claire?
    Do you feel better, Claire?

c) Pierre va se coucher le plus **lentement/honnêtement** possible.
    Pierre is going to go to bed as slowly as possible.

d) Cette robe te va **bien/mieux** que l'autre.
    That dress suits you better than the other one.

e) Le bébé dort **mieux/lentement** maintenant.
    The baby is sleeping better now.

Yes, much better,
thanks — and now
totally dandruff-free!

Mieux means better. It doesn't look anything like bien, though.

Subject Pronouns

Q1   Write out all of the French sentences from List A.
Next to each one, write the right English translation from List B.

List A

a) Elle te téléphonera demain.

b) Ils ont tous les deux 8 ans.

c) Il est médecin.

d) Est-ce que tu as vu mes baskets?

e) Où sont-elles?

f) Elle est au garage.

List B

Where are they?

He's a doctor.

She will phone you tomorrow.

It is at the garage.

They are both 8 years old.

Have you seen my trainers?

Q2   Write out all the sentences a) to e). There's a pronoun (a **he/she** or **they** word) missing from the second sentence in each one. Use your incredible skill and judgement to fill it in.

Jeanne est professeur. ⟹ **<u>Elle</u> va chaque jour au collège**

Jeanne is a teacher.   <u>She</u> goes to school every day.

a) Mon père ne travaille pas. .... est au chômage.

b) Ma souris est malade. .... ne mange rien.

c) Leur père est mécanicien. .... travaille dans un garage.

d) Mes soeurs sont jumelles. .... ont toutes les deux 15 ans.

e) Ses parents sont en vacances. .... rentrent à la maison la semaine prochaine.

f) Mes amies sont en ville.   ... m'attendent devant le cinéma.

You need il, elle, ils and elles.

Q3   In each of these sentences, there's a choice between using **tu** or **vous**.
Write them all out in French, using the right one.

a) "Hi, Dad, how are you"
*Bonjour, Papa, comment **allez-vous** / **vas-tu**?*

b) Asking a teacher — "Could you close the window please?"
***Pouvez-vous** / **peux-tu** fermer la fenêtre, **s'il vous plaît**/ **s'il te plaît**?*

c) Asking someone in the street — "Excuse me, what is the time?"
***Excusez-moi**/ **Excuse-moi**, quelle heure est-il, **s'il vous plaît** / **s'il te plaît**?*

d) Talking to a friend on the phone — "Have you seen that film already?"
*Est-ce que **vous avez** / **tu as** déja vu ce film?*

e) Arranging to meet friends in town — "Where will you be at 7pm"
*Où **serez-vous** / **seras-tu** à dix-neuf heures?*

Remember, tu is for a person you know well, and vous is for being polite, or for several people.

Watch out — you need vous for <u>more than one person</u>, even if they're all your mates.

Possessive Adjectives

Q1 Write these sentences out in full. You'll need to choose the right option from the two words in bold each time. Use the English translation to point you in the right direction.

eg <u>**Ma**</u> *maison est grande.*

<u>My</u> house is big.

eg <u>**Sa**</u> *soeur est étudiante.*

<u>His/her</u> sister is a student.

It's <u>always</u> sa, because <u>sister</u> is feminine. It doesn't make a blind bit of difference whether the person whose sister it is is male or female.

a) **Mon/Ma** vélo est rouge.   *My bicycle is red*

b) **Soi/Son** chat est malade.   *Her cat is ill*

c) **Son/Sa** mère habite en France.   *His mother lives in France.*

d) Je n'ai pas fait **mon/mes** devoirs.   *I haven't done my homework.*

e) Est-ce que tu as vu **mon/ton** argent?   *Have you seen my money?*

f) As-tu parlé à **ta/ton** soeur?   *Did you speak to your sister?*

Q2 Write these sentences out in full. You'll need to choose the right option from the two words at the end each time. Use the English translation to point you in the right direction.

eg <u>**Nos**</u> *bananes sont vertes.*

<u>Our</u> bananas are green.

eg *Je connais <u>leur</u> père.*

I know <u>their</u> dad.

a) Où avons-nous garé .... voiture?   **nos**   **notre**
   Where did we park our car?

b) Ils ont perdu .... sacs.   **ses**   **leurs**
   They have lost their bags.

c) .... élèves sont très sages.   **vos**   **votres**
   Your pupils are very well behaved.

d) As-tu déja rencontré .... frère?   **leur**   **son**
   Have you ever met their brother?

e) J'ai acheté .... cadeaux.   **leur**   **leurs**
   I have bought their presents.

f) .... cousin Phil est en vacances.   **notre**   **nos**
   Our cousin Phil is on holiday.

Q3 Translate these sentences into French. Any tricky French words are given in the oval. You need to figure out whether each sentence needs **ma**, **sa**, **son**, **votre** or whatever.

a) Where is my homework?

b) I met my friends.

c) His girlfriend is very nice.

d) Where is your (a person you know well 'you') house?

homework — devoirs
girlfriend — petite amie

Emphatic Pronouns

Q1   Write out these sentences and underline the pronouns.

eg *Il est plus grand que toi.* ⟹ *Il est plus grand que <u>toi</u>.*

a) Il est plus grand que toi.
b) Je t'envoie une photo de lui.
c) Il est moins sympa qu'elle.
d) Je vais me promener avec vous.
e) Elle est triste sans lui!

f) Vous êtes plus rapides que nous!
g) Il a peur de nous.
h) Tu as quelque chose pour moi?
i) Nous sommes plus nombreux que vous.
j) Mon frère est plus petit que toi.

Q2   Write out French sentences a) to f) filling in each gap with the right pronoun from the table.

	je	tu	il / elle	nous	vous	ils
Pronouns ⟹	moi	toi	lui / elle	nous	vous	eux

eg *He is always late!* ⟹ *Lui, il est toujours en retard!*

Hint: look at the word that comes after the comma and then find the pronoun that matches it.

a) At least she knows what she wants.
b) At least we are always there on time.
c) As for me, I don't know.
d) You are always right, aren't you!
e) You (plural) are really starting to annoy me!
f) They (masculine) will just eat vegetables.

.... , *elle sait ce qu'elle veut.*
........, *nous sommes toujours à l'heure.*
.... , *je ne sais pas.*
.... , *tu as toujours raison!*
.... , *vous commencez à m'énerver!*
.... , *ils mangeront des légumes.*

Q3   Turn these bossy French sentences into English ones.

eg *Levez-vous, la classe!* ⟹ *Stand up, class!*

a) Ecoutez-moi bien, les élèves!
b) Habille-toi vite, on est en retard!
c) Tais-toi, tu fais trop de bruit!

d) Lave-toi vite!
e) Regarde-moi pour la photo!
f) Donnez-moi vos habits sales!

Chewy Vocab	
élèves	students / pupils
se taire	be quiet
bruit	noise
habit	clothes
sale	dirty

Regarde-moi pour la photo!

Pronoun Word Order

Q1 Each of these English sentences has two French versions beside it. One of them's right, the other one's wrong. Write out the English sentence with the right French version.

1) She can see him there.   Elle l'y voit. / Elle y le voit.

2) I am buying him it.   Je le lui achète. / Lui je le achète.

3) My mother is giving you some.   Ma mère donne en toi. / Ma mère t'en donne.

4) He is showing me them.   Il me les montre. / Il les mes montre.

5) She is selling it (feminine) to us.   Nous la elle vend. / Elle nous la vend.

6) She is meeting them there.   Elle les y rencontre. / Elle y les rencontre.

7) You are buying him some.   Vous en lui achetez. / Vous lui en achetez.

Q2 Follow the example and write out negative versions of sentences a) - h).

eg *Je les mange* ⟹ *Je **ne** les mange **pas**.*

    I eat them.   I don't eat them.

You won't have to write these often, but it helps to know what they mean.

a) Il les voit.

b) Nous la regardons.

c) Je l'y rencontre ce soir.

d) Il me dit tout.

e) Vous le lui rendez demain.

f) Tu me le dois.

g) Je lui en veux.

h) Elle lui doit dix francs.

Cake Scully?

No thanks, I don't eat them. I'm watching my figure.

Q3 Write out these French sentences and put the English meaning next to them.

All these sentences are in the perfect tense by the way.

a) Je vous l'ai donné.   **We met him / her there last week.**

b) Nous les y avons mangées.   **They never brought you them.**

c) Vous en êtes revenus quand?   **You gave me them for my birthday.**

d) Tu nous en a parlé?   **When did you come back from there?**

e) Elle la lui a rendue.   **We ate them there.**

f) Je te les ai rendus hier.   **I gave them back to you yesterday.**

g) Nous l'y avons rencontré la semaine dernière.   **She gave it back to her / him.**

h) Tu me les a offerts pour mon anniversaire.   **I have given you it.**

i) Ils ne te les ont jamais apportés.   **Have you talked to us about it?**

Demonstrative Adjectives and Pronouns

Q1 These look a bit trickier, but if you make sure you know the gender of the word, and follow the examples, you should be fine. Write out these nouns with **ce**, **cet**, **cette** or **ces**.

eg **ce chapeau**
this hat

cet anorak
this anorak

cette jupe
this skirt

ces chaussures
these shoes

Ce, cet, and cette all mean 'this'. Ces means 'these'.

a) .... maison
b) .... orange
c) .... chapeau
d) .... chaussettes
e) .... moustique

f) ...... enfant
g) ....chiens
h) ....nouvelle
i) ....éléphant
J) ....chocolat

Hats for All Occasions

This hat, sir?

Q2 Each of these French sentences a) to d) has two options to fill in the gap. Use the box to help you decide which is the right one and write out the whole sentence.

Singular		Plural	
Masculine	Feminine	Masculine	Feminine
celui	celle	ceux	celles

eg *J'ai deux chiens. Celui-ci est mignon, mais .... est méchant.*

⟹ *J'ai deux chiens. Celui-ci est mignon, mais **celui-là** est méchant.*

I have two dogs. This one is sweet, but that one is naughty.

When a pronoun has -ci after it, it means 'this one (here)' and if it has -là after it, it means 'that one (there)'.

a) Donne-moi un stylo. Pas celui-là, ..., devant moi. **celle-ci / celui-ci**
Give me a pen. Not that one, this one, in front of me.

b) Voici des cahiers. .... ne sont vieux, mais ceux-là sont tout neufs! **celui-ci / ceux-ci**
Here are the exercise books. These ones are old, but those ones are brand new.

c) Voici les robes. Celle-ci est à ma soeur, mais .... est à moi! **celle-là / celles-là**
Here are the dresses. This one is for my sister, but that one is for me!

d) Regarde ces fleurs! .... sont très belles, mais celles-là sont encore plus jolies! **ceux-ci / celles-ci**

Look at the flowers. These ones are very beautiful, but those ones are even prettier.

Answers

Section 1 — Topics

1 Q1 a) 4 b) 9 c) 11 d) 18 e) 20 f) 14

Q2 a) un b) sept c) huit d) quatorze e) cent neuf f) trente-cinq g) dix-sept h) soixante et onze i) soixante-trois j) cinq cent quatre-vingt-un k) trois cent quatre-vingt-douze l) cinq mille quatre cent trente-et-un m) dix-neuf cent quatre-vingt-trois OR mille neuf cent quatre-vingt-trois. n) deux mille quatre o) dix-neuf cent quatre-vingt-dix-neuf OR mille neuf cent quatre-vingt-dix-neuf. p) un million

Q3 a) dixième b) septième c) premier/première (fem) d) deuxième e) quatre-vingtième f) deux centième

Q4 a) cent vingt-cinq euros b) quatre-vingt-neuf euros et cinquante cents c) deux cent dix euros d) cent quarante-neuf euros et quatre-vingt quinze cents.

2 Q1 a) some b) several c) every/each d) all the (masculine) e) many/ a lot of f) all the (feminine) g) few h) others

Q2 a) Every man is wearing a hat. b) All the supermarkets are open on Sunday. c) I saw a lot of young people at the shopping centre. d) He came with some friends e) I've read this book several times.

Q3 a) souvent often b) rarement rarely c) quelquefois sometimes d) toujours always

Q4 a) Quelquefois, je joue de la guitare. b) Je mange souvent de la pizza.

3 Q1 a) When Quand b) Why Pourquoi c) Where Où d) Who Qui e) How Comment f) How many Combien g) What Qu'est-ce que h) Which Quels

Q2 a) Do you have any brothers or sisters? b) How are you? c) What are you doing tomorrow afternoon? d) How many apples are there here? e) Where are my trousers? f) When is he going to arrive?

Q3 a) Quand b) Où c) Qu'est-ce que d) Qui e) Pourquoi

4 Q1 a) Lisez la liste = Read the list b) Répondez aux questions = Answer the questions c) Tournez la page = Turn the page d) Voici un exemple = Here is an example e) Repondez en français = Answer in French f) D'abord = First, ...

Q2 a) Write the letter of the word that matches the picture. b) Find the symbol that goes with the word. c) You won't need all the letters. d) You can use a dictionary if you want to. e) Draw an arrow to show which picture goes with which caption. f) Fill in the grid. g) Answer in French or tick the boxes. h) Tick the right boxes. i) Look at the grid.

5 Q1 a) Hi! b) Fifteen c) Martine d) Policeman e) Dentist f) Physics and Geography g) It's very hard and his teacher is too strict h) Bordeaux

Q2 Letter must include all five points, in proper French.

6 Q1 a) Get up! b) Sit down! c) Be quiet! d) Be quiet! e) Give me your exercise book f) Lend me your pen g) Listen to me! h) Write that in your exercise books! i) Stop!

Q2 a) Excusez-moi, monsieur b) Je m'excuse! c) Comment allez-vous? d) De rien e) Je suis désolé(e) f) Enchanté(e)

7 Q1 Likes are a), b), e). f), g) and h) . Dislikes are c) and d)

Q2 Je trouve Charles gentil. Je trouve Laurent affreux. Je trouve Sophie ennuyeuse. Je le trouve formidable.

8 Q1 a) beautiful = beau/belle b) interesting = intéressant(e) c) great = chouette d) excellent = excellent(e) e) bad = mauvais(e) f) friendly = amical(e)

Q2 Answers should all start Je pense que, and use a word from the box in a way that makes sense.

Q3 a) Je trouve les OuestBoyz excellents, parce qu'ils chantent bien. b) Jean-Pierre est fatigué parce qu'il a beaucoup travaillé. c) Je ne peux pas sortir ce soir, parce que j'ai trop de devoirs à faire. d) Marie ne va pas acheter ces chaussures parce qu'elles sont trop chères.

9 Q1 a) 4 b) 3 c) 6 d) 2 e) 1 f) 5

Q2 a) Il pleut. = It's raining. b) Il fait du vent. = It's windy. c) Il y a des éclairs. = There's lightning. d) Il fait beau. = It is fine. e) Il fait froid. = It's cold. f) Il fait chaud. = It's hot.

Q3 a) It will be cold. b) It will be windy. c) It will be sunny. d) It will snow. e) There will be clouds. f) It will rain.

Q4 a) It was sunny. b) There was fog. c) The weather was bad. OR It was dull. d) It was fine. e) It was raining. f) There was lightning.

10 Q1 l'Italie l'Autriche l'Afrique l'Écosse les Pays-Bas l'Espagne l'Europe le pays de Galles l'Allemagne les États-Unis la Belgique l'Irlande du Nord l'Amérique la France la Grande-Bretagne

Q2 a) Je suis irlandais(e) b) Je suis hollandais(e) c) Je suis écossais(e) d) Je suis anglais(e) f) Je suis allemand(e) f) Je suis gallois(e)

Q3 Answers should follow the pattern given.

11 Q1 partir = to leave; la pension complète = full board; la nuit = night; la demi-pension = half board; une chambre simple = single room; une auberge = guest house; rester = to stay; la personne = person; le camping = campsite; réserver = to reserve; coûter = to cost; une auberge de jeunesse = youth hostel; les vacances = holidays; la chambre double = double room; la place = space available; un hôtel = hotel

Q2 a) 8 b) 5 c) 8 people d) It's communal

12 Q1 a) Welcome to the Champs du Soleil (Sunny Fields) campsite. Spaces for 30 tents and 15 caravans. b) It is forbidden to light fires here. c) Drinking water. d) Showers - ladies/gentlemen. e) You can hire sleeping bags here.

Q2 a) C b) B c) D d) A

13 Q1 a) B b) A c) A

Q2 a) Quarter past two (in the morning). b) No. c) Coffee and a sandwich. d) Breakfast starts at 7:30am and finishes at 10am. e) Lunch starts at 12pm, and finishes at 3pm. f) By 11am.

14 Q1 a) la boucherie b) l'hôpital c) la bibliothèque d) le château e) la pâtisserie f) le supermarché g) le restaurant h) la boulangerie i) l'aéroport j) le zoo k) la poste l) la piscine m) le syndicat d'initiative n) l'église o) le cinéma p) l'école

Q2 a) Je vais à la banque pour changer de l'argent. b) Hier soir j'ai vu une très jolie pièce au théatre. c) On peut voir des objets très vieux faits par les gens d'autrefois au musée. d) Je voudrais acheter de l'aspirine. Est-ce qu'il y a une pharmacie près d'ici?

15 Q1 c)